OUTCOME MEASURES AND EVALUATION

IN COUNSELLING AND PSYCHOTHERAPY

OUTCOME MEASURES AND EVALUATION

IN COUNSELLING AND PSYCHOTHERAPY

BY
CHRIS EVANS AND
JO-ANNE CARLYLE

SAGE

Los Angeles | London | New Delhi
Singapore | Washington DC | Melbourne

SAGE

Los Angeles | London | New Delhi
Singapore | Washington DC | Melbourne

SAGE Publications Ltd
1 Oliver's Yard
55 City Road
London EC1Y 1SP

SAGE Publications Inc.
2455 Teller Road
Thousand Oaks, California 91320

SAGE Publications India Pvt Ltd
B 1/I 1 Mohan Cooperative Industrial Area
Mathura Road
New Delhi 110 044

SAGE Publications Asia-Pacific Pte Ltd
3 Church Street
#10-04 Samsung Hub
Singapore 049483

Editor: Susannah Trefgarne
Assistant editor: Ruth Lilly
Production editor: Manmeet Kaur Tura
Copyeditor: Sarah Bury
Proofreader: Clare Weaver
Marketing manager: Dilhara Attygalle
Cover design: Sheila Tong
Typeset by: C&M Digitals (P) Ltd, Chennai, India
Printed in the UK

Library of Congress Control Number: 2021941862

British Library Cataloguing in Publication data

A catalogue record for this book is available from the British Library

ISBN 978-1-4739-0672-3
ISBN 978-1-4739-0673-0 (pbk)

At SAGE we take sustainability seriously. Most of our products are printed in the UK using responsibly sourced papers and boards. When we print overseas we ensure sustainable papers are used as measured by the PREPS grading system. We undertake an annual audit to monitor our sustainability.

Contents

List of Figures and Tables

List of Figures

List of Tables

About the Authors

Chris Evans is a Visiting Professor at the Universities of UDLA, Ecuador and Sheffield, UK. He trained in medicine and psychiatry, specialising in psychotherapy with trainings in individual analytic therapy, group analysis and family/systemic therapy. He always combined research with clinical work and his driving interest has been "how is it that we think we know what it is that we think we know?" ... which he admits may have been a bit generic for a really focused research career! However, it drove wide exploration of research and assessment methods, led him to co-create the CORE system (www.coresystemtrust.org.uk) and to co-lead over 30 translations of CORE instruments. He co-authored the first paper naming "practice based evidence": as a vital complement to "evidence-based practice": one theme of this book. He is now a full-time freelance researcher holding personal chairs in Sheffield, UK and Quito, Ecuador.

Jo-anne Carlyle is the Director, PSYCTC.com. Jo-anne trained in clinical and forensic psychology, psychoanalytic psychotherapy, research and organisational consultancy. She has worked in health, education and third sector settings and has expertise in delivery of clinical services; leadership development and strategy; professional regulation and governance; research; development and delivery of psychotherapy training, project management and outcome monitoring. Her consulting work has been in the UK, Canada, Ecuador, India and Lithuania, as well as internationally online. She has an interest in humanitarian and development work and is transitioning her activities to projects with more social impact. She currently sits as a non-executive director on education and charity boards.

Acknowledgements

No new knowledge emerges in a vacuum: between us we have over 75 years of interest in and working with clinical research and measurement tools and our ideas about them have been honed over that time and sharpened through conversations with clients, with students and with colleagues. We share a healthy scepticism for the reification of theoretical concepts and psychological instruments, but we also share a belief that when used well and thoughtfully they can be transformative, especially if used in a spirit of collaborative enquiry. We believe this is a route to more sophisticated and relevant understandings of the work we do in counselling and psychotherapy and in evaluating the effectiveness of that work.

The journey to writing this book has been somewhat slow and many people provided valuable input and assistance along the route who we would like to thank. As a series editor for SAGE, Andrew Reeves initially invited us to contribute to this book and played a key role in its commissioning and development. Susannah Trefgarne, Ruth Lilly and their colleagues at Sage have remained steadfast in support of the book, despite our time keeping; and Manmeet Kaur Tura has provided a supportive presence through the production process. Three anonymous reviewers provided valuable feedback on the manuscript. We would particularly like to voice our appreciation to the following colleagues for their generosity in dedicating their time and careful reflections on earlier drafts of chapters: Lila Adana, Jan Baker, Emily Blackshaw, Maggy Cairns, Frank Dwyer, Xavier Eloquin, Marija Farrugia, Janet Fernando, Wayne Full, Aasra Garrib, Alicia Georgiades, Susan McPherson, Daniel Moerken, Clara Paz, Caroline Phillips, Cynthia Rogers, Pablo Sabucedo, Chris Scanlon, Cordet Smith, Janet Smithson, Adriana Svacina, Chris Tanner, Adriana Trujillo, Elizabeth Weightman and Sula Yassin.

Finally, special thanks go to Randall Munroe for kind permission to reproduce a number of his amazing xkcd cartoons that put the heart into maths and statistics. To see more of these go to: xkcd.com

Introduction: how to read this book

The road map

Who is the book for? Clearly it is aimed at counsellors and psychotherapists who wish to know more about 'outcome measurement', but feedback has told us that it has a relevance to others: health professionals, service managers, postgraduate students, organisational consultants and all those who are interested in looking at the impact of interventions. The ideas come from some universal questions: What are the different ways of being able to be confident in what we know? How can we understand change? For us, these questions touch on wider philosophical and scientific questions that will be helpful to revisit to understand what might be useful to whom.

Starting point and destination

Chapters 1 and 10 each act as 'book-ends' that can be read as a linked duo. They may actually be enough for some audiences: managers, commissioners, counsellors and therapists who do not wish to use outcome measures themselves but who want to understand what is involved when talking to other practitioners or reading research papers.

For everyone else, we think all of the book should be of value but recognise that people will have very different starting points in terms of their familiarity with therapy (as clients, therapists or both) as well as their experiences with measurement, research, audit, commissioning and supervision. What follows is a brief guide to what the book offers.

Part I, Chapter 1, gives an overview and introduction to Outcome Measurement (OM). It sets out why we think OM is relevant for all therapies: as particular lens to try to understand and improve our practice. In case that sounds starry eyed, we also believe there are some real limitations to OM and that it is over-valued in some quarters, and so we give a pragmatic, grounded approach to its benefits and limitations.

Following this overview, Part II, Chapters 2 to 5, get into the practicalities of how to choose measures and how to digest the data from outcome measures. These chapters should also be useful to people reading outcome reports and research who may not yet intend to conduct their own projects. Chapter 2 sets out the foundations from which using OM in therapy has developed. Everyone is familiar with measurement in some form and we try to locate OM in systems that will be familiar to people, with a view to exploring some of the conceptual issues that underpin measurement and evidence. We highlight the different audiences for outcome measurement (clients, professionals, commissioners) and debunk some myths about the methods. Chapter 3 explores how to judge the quality of measures. Although this includes powerful, perhaps totemic words like 'reliability' and 'validity', we look particularly at generalisability, usability, linguistics and cultural location, as well as giving an introduction to psychometrics.

Chapter 4 gives frameworks for evaluating measures and starts to address the practicalities of using measures routinely. Chapter 5 introduces the kinds of statistical procedures you need to understand when reading reports or research papers or analysing your own data. For many people, statistics can be alienating but as soon as you have more numbers than you can hold in your mind at one time, procedures to summarise, categorise and simplify them are vital and these are what statistical methods do. In this chapter we walk you through ways to summarise data and we introduce you to key tools and concepts you will find in outcome measure reports.

Part III focuses on collecting and using outcome data and embeds this within the conversations that underpin good data use or project development. This section depends on the foundations set out in Part II and we strongly recommend that you digest Part II before rolling your sleeves up and getting stuck in. Chapter 6 underlines that design and logistics are vital and gives practical advice on ensuring your data will be meaningful. It offers guidance to avoid the common errors which can be hard, or impossible, to undo after you have started. Most people underestimate the importance of careful planning and we encourage you to set aside more time for this planning stage than you expect to need. The more you get things in good order here, the more valuable your findings will be: 'quality in equals quality out'. Chapters 7 and 8 are worked examples of different outcome measurement projects with Chapter 7 focusing on two imaginary individual practitioners and Chapter 8 a single large service. Chapter 9 brings us back to the relational: how to work with outcome measures with clients and in supervision.

It uses familiar scenarios to give a platform to talk about measures as they are used in the therapy room and in practice.

Finally, Part IV, again a single chapter, takes us back to the importance of communication and includes tools and ideas to support you to critique outcome data effectively. Along with Chapter 1 we hope this summarises what outcome measurement can and cannot do. Chapter 10 aims to equip you to be able to stay in dialogue with people who either over-value or under-value outcome measurement. It is a guide to critique at its best, giving information that helps you to question and challenge when you meet dogmatic views, and tools to keep a conversation going. All this is in the service of that key aspiration: understanding and investing in things that can improve the services we offer to people who need them.

We hope that our approach opens the door to people who are interested in outcome measurement and supports those who have not yet had the tools, resources or confidence to make a start.

Glossary and Online Resources

We explain many technical terms in the text but we have also compiled an online glossary and a range of additional resources (https://www.psyctc.org/psyctc/book/), so do check there for terms that may be unfamiliar. Some of the figures are dense and there are colour versions, and larger, versions of the graphs with details on the simulations behind those. Finally, there is a developing compilation of online resources (e.g. confidence interval calculators), linked to the chapters and designed to help you explore your own data, and to come in helpful when reading quantitative reports.

PART I

OUTCOME MEASURES AND EVALUATION

1

An introduction to outcome measures and evaluation

So, you are thinking about using outcome measures? Perhaps you are working in a service that requires you to use them; perhaps you are interested in seeing how clients change; perhaps you want to feel more confident when talking to researchers and commissioners about clients' change. There are many reasons why someone might have picked up this book and we hope that in it you will find some useful pointers to the things you need to bear in mind when using Outcome Measures/Measurement (OM from here on). We also hope you will find sound advice about how to think critically about the pros and cons of OM.

We start with key questions: Why bother? What are the political, therapeutic and epistemological contexts for OM? Is it really do-able? What are the myths and realities to bear in mind?

Why bother?

We know that few people on their deathbeds will wish they had spent more time collecting outcome data with their clients and no one will have a single 'number' that they believe to be the 'outcome' of their lives. However, simple outcome data can be transformative. Here are some examples.

- In the 19th century Semmelweis showed simple handwashing could cut horrific post-operative death rates.

- Florence Nightingale's use of outcomes data demonstrated the effectiveness of her reforms in the Crimea and forced the government to set up a Royal Commission with the power to change policy.
- Ernest Codman coined the term 'end result' to describe his practice of following up medically and surgically treated patients for long enough to find out whether the interventions were successful and to investigate factors involved in failures as well as successes.

We use these early physical healthcare examples partly because many of the methods now being used in the psychological realm were developed in physical healthcare or other physical science domains. We try to neither idealise nor reject 'natural' sciences. Those domains have many methods we cannot or should not use, including some that are currently overused in our sphere, but they also have methods that can be really valuable for us and open up the ways we understand our work. We aim to show which are which.

We do recommend following these flag bearers who understood the value of systematic observation, good forethought and design, who used simple variables but who knew that you often have to push against the *status quo* and political pressures to make progress. While being pragmatic enough to draw on methods from outside psychological therapies, we also need to value what is special about our discipline. Psychotherapy and counselling involve the unique, the personal, the relational. So, can we bring this and outcome measurement together? Let us do that right here:

Figure 1.1 xkcd cartoon: boyfriend

Reproduced by kind permission of xkcd.com

We think this lovely cartoon from xkcd captures some of the tensions and possibilities that many therapists feel about looking at relational work with OM: sometimes it might look like numbers are over-simplifying but these numbers can be potent. Measures *can* be applied to relational uniqueness and the deeply personal in therapy!

'Outcome measurement' refers not so much about an outcome but about change: whether change has taken place between the start and the end of a process, as such outcome measurement often usefully considers points in between. These measures might be collected from the first and last sessions of therapy or perhaps at weekly intervals. In psychological therapies it is almost never meaningful to comment on the outcome (Codman's 'end-result') if you do not know something about the starting state. The different terms and acronyms in the field are sometimes confusing and 'outcome' itself is a little grandiose or misleading. It can imply that the most important thing in a therapy is whether there has been a change in scores on measures from the beginning to the end of therapy. Clearly this is not the case, as any client will tell you. However, the term is in such common use that we retained it. In Box 1.1 you will see how we will use the various relevant terms throughout the book.

BOX 1.1 Key Terms

OM: Outcome Measures/Outcome Measurement
We will use OM to refer to both the actual measures and how they are used to explore change in counselling and therapies.

ROM: Routine Outcome Measurement
We will use ROM to refer to regular use of Outcome Measures to explore change and outcomes in counselling and therapies ('routine' distinguishes it from specific research use). ROM generally aims to learn from local data but ideally also contributes to a developing pool of change data from many services. In such ROM, the data may or may not be shared between client and therapist but the aim is not to use the scores to change the process of the therapy.

EM: Embedded Measures/Measurement
Looking at measures *within* the therapy, as part of the therapy, has been common in cognitive behavioural therapy (CBT) and some family therapies for decades and is designed to help both client and therapist to monitor change, but it does not generally draw comparisons with data from other therapies.

ECM: Embedded Change Measurement
We will use ECM to describe the process when OMs are completed *within* the therapy, as in EM above, but in which the scores are given substantial weight to steer the therapy using referential data from other therapies, often designating change within this therapy as 'on track' or 'off track'. Some people use the terms 'routine outcome measurement/management/monitoring' for this but we prefer 'ECM' as a more precise term.

Sometimes people complain that OM does not reflect the depth and subtlety of what goes on between a client and therapist. Of course not! The reasons for collecting OM data are different from the reasons for doing clinical work. Clinical work is about alleviating distress, helping individuals. ROM throws some light on whether and how much clients attending a service change over time, whether treatments are effective. It is important not to confuse or conflate the two: they intersect but are different.

The use of OMs has developed over the last 100 years, partly through the expansion of psychometrics (literally 'measurement of psychological matters') and the emergence of ways to assess the qualities of the measures used. With this, multi-item rating scales came to dominate OMs. We will come back to psychometric evaluation of OMs in Chapter 3 as psychometric methods are a valuable way to criticise and test the robustness of OM findings. Constructive critique is something we return to throughout the book but particularly in Chapter 10, as we believe no information is of real use unless its strengths and weaknesses are explored. However, critique can become rigid and psychometric methods are not immune from this, so we try to give a balanced appraisal of those tools.

No evidence is equally available to all, nor is it ever equally persuasive to all. The importance of the audience for OM data is another theme we return to throughout the book. OM data is often seen as 'research' and venerated or denigrated by some because of this. Our aim is to make OM data usefully available to clients, potential clients and therapists rather than particularly to 'researchers'. There is an argument used by some clinicians that 'every session is a research project'. We have some sympathy with the sentiment behind this, and with well-designed single case studies (n = 1 experiments), and we believe that large n samples are often overvalued in our field. However, this argument is often used to simply reject OM and quantitative research.

So what is research? Dictionary definitions have research as the systematic study of something in order to develop understanding and reach new conclusions. We argue that for work to be research, not only must it answer a question, or at least improve upon the question, it must also be shared: good research solves problems or clarifies our understanding of problems for a wider audience. Any therapy may improve things for the client, and the therapist will always learn something new from the work. However, unless the learning is shared with others it is not research. Therapies are generally private and confidential and using OMs in them, though valuable, does not make the therapy research, any more than new understanding from your last session or your last client is research. However, whether it is formal research or not, appropriate sharing of data out of therapies allows critique and shared learning and this book is about *all* ways of doing that, not just those designated as research.

This issue of sharing learning touches on safeguarding, confidentiality and clients' autonomy to decide how their data may be used. One huge difference between therapy data and physical science data turns on this ethical issue: physical science objects of exploration do not have rights over their data, clients do. One appeal of OM data is that it simplifies some of the challenges here as a score on a measure will not leak a client's identity.

We believe that any therapist can make valuable use of OMs and of using them routinely: ROM (see Box 1.1) gives therapists the easiest way to bridge across from the necessary confidentiality of the therapy session to wider organisational and cultural audiences. Throughout the book we will look at such data sharing but also at change measurement within sessions (EM and ECM - see Box 1.1), but before we do this, we should look at the wider picture and connections to the external world:

1. What can ROM and OM offer when used in appropriate contexts?
2. How does this help explain why we should engage with them?

We think there are political, curiosity/knowledge-led and therapeutic answers to these questions.

Political reasons for OM/ROM

These have been dominant since around 1990 as public sector funding globally is increasingly tied to 'evidence'. In the UK, NICE (National Institute for Health and Care Excellence) guidelines mean that psychotherapy modalities that are not seen to have an evidence base are unlikely to be funded. 'Third sector' organisations and EAPs (Employee Assistance Programmes) also increasingly require OMs, although with some freedom to learn from mistakes that the public sector often makes with ROM. Practitioners working in these sectors will find themselves using OMs and so need to understand them.

At least as important as that overt political need is public opinion. People - potential and actual clients - are increasingly more literate about evidence, more numerate about data, and access a wide range of media when they are seeking interventions. Many will choose therapies based on the evidence they can find about outcomes. Way before the internet, it was Codman's belief that patients should be able to find 'end result' data about surgical and medical options that drove his creation of 'end result cards', pioneering ROM data. It is important that counsellors and therapists feel able to discuss the outcome evidence when clients ask about it. Clients' questions may be generic, or they may also ask about your own, or your service's, evidence about change. Of course, most clients are also looking for a therapist whom they feel they can trust and work well with, but questions about outcome data may be part of testing that. We hope this book will help you to find sensible ways to respond to these questions, to collect your own change/outcome data and feed it constructively into these wider systems.

Knowledge-led reasons for OM/ROM

Keats famously asserted:

> Beauty is truth, truth beauty, — that is all
>
> Ye know on earth, and all ye need to know. (Keats, 1819)

Keats did not put philosophers out of business, and for them this is 'epistemology': how we think we know what we think we know. It touches all ways that 'truth' and 'evidence' are understood and when evidence is persuasive.

OM data have provided crucial evidence in psychological therapies as the use of measures in psychology, psychotherapy and counselling exploded through the 20th and early 21st centuries. That explosion was mainly in the epistemological framework of empirical positivism: that is, the view that the 'truth' is out there and that good reasoning and empirical research reveals it. In much the same historical period, empirical positivism was largely abandoned in the natural sciences, and confidence about 'falsifiability' and about complete and testable models was renounced. In maths and nuclear physics respectively, Gödel's incompleteness theorems and the Heisenberg/Yukawa uncertainty principle destroyed the confident positivist framework when Gödel showed that areas of number theory could never be complete and entirely internally coherent, and Heisenberg and Yukawa showed that the idea that everything about any particle could be measured simultaneously and to any level of precision was impossible.

Given the power of the physical sciences as a paradigm for all 'sciences', it is worth understanding this revolution. Einstein's initial reaction to the uncertainty principle is said to have been 'God wouldn't play dice with the universe', but he came to accept the evidence as overwhelming. That framework led another Nobel prize winner, Niels Bohr, to proclaim:

> Physics is to be regarded not so much as the study of something a priori given, but rather as the development of methods of ordering and surveying human experience. In this respect our task must be to account for such experience in a manner independent of individual subjective judgement and therefore objective in the sense that it can be unambiguously communicated in ordinary human language. (Bohr, 1963: 10)

Bohr's idea of eliminating 'individual subjective judgement' is not possible for the measurement of human experiences but it is interesting to see a 'hard scientist' framing evidence as being about the 'development of methods of ordering and surveying human experience'. If we substitute 'respecting but minimising individual subjective judgement' for his 'independent of individual subjective judgement' we feel we have a useful game plan for monitoring therapies. In this, ROM is not about the positivist aim of finding truth 'out there', but is about 'the development of methods of ordering and surveying human experience'.

Perhaps it was psychology's fight for status as a fledgling science that meant it clung to the empirical positivist tradition through the early 20th century while most natural sciences abandoned this. In the late 20th century large swathes of psychology and therapies then swung correctively and passionately into postmodernism and social constructionism: the arguments that understandings of the world are co-constructed, determined by their historical, cultural, social and political context and shaped by power relationships. This swing was often linked with extreme rejection of any measurement models. We believe it is time to move beyond this increasingly sterile stand off. We are clear that there are certainly no universally and demonstrably correct meta-theories of the mind, but we like to adopt the pragmatism of most natural sciences without pretending we have their measurements and without losing faith that human experience, not non-living entities, is at the heart of our field.

In this model, our 'epistemological position' is: 'what is it that persuades you that you can make assertions about what is true, or about what seems usefully applicable?' and we believe that thoughtful use of OMs can lead to better models and improved practices.

One example of the use of OM data that changed practice concerns the offering of therapies following sudden, particularly shared, trauma. An increasingly solid body of OM data shows that offering uniform intervention to everyone immediately after a traumatic event is largely unhelpful. Such interventions had arisen from the plausible idea that after trauma the opportunity to talk will be useful. However, the data showed a complicated picture in which this is far from always the case. As the data built, a new understanding emerged: that for those lucky enough to have them, access to normal support networks (family and friends) is far more important than professional help, but also that, even for those who do not have good support or internal resilience, early intervention can undermine normal coping strategies. It is where and when these basic core strategies do not work, and for the subgroup of people *not* recovering, that therapists can offer help and almost certainly that is when it becomes efficient and effective to do so.

This demonstrates two ideas central to using OM data. Firstly, we need to be open to where our therapies may not be effective or may even cause harm. If we hold this brave openness, we can explore the complexities that may be operating, and be better fitted to adapt and change. Secondly, good outcome evaluation needs the input of both practitioners and clients to identify the areas that are really relevant to therapeutic change in order to hone our measures appropriately: knowledge comes with valuing everyone's experience, not just professional expertise.

OK, let us leave the philosophy and come back to the pragmatics and our third reason for using OMs.

Therapeutic reasons for OM/ROM

We do believe that good use of OMs can help the development of therapy generically. However, let us come at this backwards: sadly, one of the reasons for writing this book is that OM data are too often over-valued and presented as magically able to distinguish between ineffective and effective therapies. This is not true: there is no such panacea. ROM has real strengths and can help address the now near cliché question: 'what works for whom?', but there is no magic answer to that incredibly complicated question either generically: 'x therapy is better than y', nor specifically: 'x will work for Jessie Smith'. To use OMs to help improve therapy we must counter this idealisation.

So OMs are not a panacea, but they really can help our work by giving us information about changes in therapy. Most counsellors and therapists chose this field because they want to be able to help their clients and to reduce distress and they use personal experience built up over years to make judgements about what helps clients. That personal experience and developing of expertise are essential but not sufficient: for the field as a whole, they need to be balanced with shared information about change.

This brings us to how both subjectivity and objectivity are vital to therapies. Subjectivity allows us to have empathy and is fundamental for clients to feel understood and less isolated. Individual clinical experience is largely subjective, narrative, interactional and emerges from collaboration with clients and is specific to our own work. However, objectivity involves taking on board others' experience and includes learning from others' quantified outcomes and, to take one example, it may help us to avoid keeping a therapeutic relationship going when evidence suggests it is time to end it.

This highlights the importance of being able to draw on both subjective and objective data to understand better how therapy works and how to use OMs. We think it is helpful to think of subjectivity and objectivity as ends of a rather complicated spectrum rather than oppositions or contradictions, even as different dimensions in a two-dimensional plane. Using this idea, we can start with the subjective experiences of clients using OMs and this reminds us that OM data arise from interactive subjective processes. If, as therapists, we give cues that we are contemptuous or sceptical of OMs, it is likely to affect how the client sees the questions. Our own experience is that clients generally engage with OMs and in interesting ways. Occasionally, clients think of measures as being a bit of a burden, but more often they are interested in the questions and are often more open to using OMs than therapists, who may fear judgements about their work.

Research into clients' experiences of measures has been a late arrival but is developing. This work suggests that service users prefer self-rated measures to clinician-rated ones and also that they feel it is important to look at both positive and negative experiences. This fits our clinical experience that clients want to be seen in their entirety - as whole people - not just in relation to their diagnosis or presenting difficulty. Feedback from service users is vital to compare OMs. For example, user involvement showed that some quality of life measures make the assumption that contact with family is necessarily a good thing. The reality is that for many, prior experiences with care givers and family may mean that sadly this is not always true. Evaluation by clients and ex-clients, 'experts by experience', highlights issues that clinicians and researchers who have not been service users might miss. Collaboration with clients is what we do clinically, and we believe that engaging with clients in research both adds to the evidence base and is congruent with good clinical practice. This is about thoughtful and collaborative use of both subjective and objective data.

OK, using OMs can be useful, but is ROM do-able?

What are the barriers?

Getting started is the first hurdle. Whether because ROM is unfamiliar or because it feels like another thing to think about when running a busy practice, there can be reluctance to start using OMs routinely. Even people trained in a 'scientist practitioner' model (for example, clinical psychologists) tend not to use OMs unless they are working in a setting with others where ROM is part of the service protocols.

Most of us need support to do things that are new to us and most of us work best when we find people with whom to collaborate. So, developing OM networks in clinics, within a professional group or with researchers will help support the use of OMs. We will talk more about this later in the book.

An internal barrier to using OMs is feeling that many widely used OM measures are alien to the theory and/or modality of certain psychotherapy and counselling approaches. Many measures were developed within CBT and psychiatric settings and these measures, though widely used, share fewer conceptual assumptions with other modalities (humanistic, psychodynamic, systemic). However, scores on different measures show strong correlations with each other despite theory differences and we believe it is no longer credible for any modality to argue that there are no measures appropriate for their work and we believe only a tiny minority of clients would accept this argument.

So, where do I start?

With this book and its guidance! Seriously, there are some broad guidelines here that will be helpful before starting to use OMs. As we will show repeatedly, they are not rocket science but, as with most new ventures, it is important to get the fundamentals in place.

The absolute fundamental if you are to use OMs is to know what you want to learn from them, but also, if you are to get the best from them, to know with whom you want to share that. Your own reasons may be political, knowledge-seeking or therapeutic, or some mix of these, but you will learn more from your data if you know what you want from your data collection.

Do the same with the question of audience: do you want to share data within a small group of like-minded practitioners you know well, or more widely? Do you want to share it with potential future clients, or perhaps make it available on web pages about your work? Does it need to be shared within your service (if you work in one)? Does it need to speak to managers or commissioners? Do you want it to speak to therapy researchers? Your choices here will be vital to guide what you choose to do. No single use of OMs or ROM will be persuasive to everyone.

Summary

In this chapter we have tried to be realistic about the barriers as well as the opportunities in using OMs and started to introduce our fundamentals: What do you want to know? How do you choose which measures to use and when? How do you ensure that your findings speak to your chosen audience? How do you then incorporate them into your practice? How do you talk to your clients about them? How would you use them in supervision? What do you need to do with the data in order to turn them into findings?

The rest of the book will set some of these issues out in more detail, but will also give you a framework within which you can plan how you might start using outcome measurement either in your own practice or with colleagues.

PART II

OUTCOME MEASURES

2

A framework for outcome measurement

To use OMs we have to have an understanding of them. This understanding links both to the context in which measures are used and also to key dimensions of the measures themselves. Whether the choice of measures is your own or is out of your hands, it is still necessary to have a framework from which you can understand where the measures are located. This chapter gives you that framework.

We will look at this from a number of vantage points but we are not yet addressing whether a measure is good or not: we will come to that in Chapter 3. Here we look at some overarching features you need to understand in order to evaluate OMs and the bigger picture of elements that make up a measure.

People coming from different backgrounds may be more or less familiar with some of the key issues we will explore. These include:

- 'Hard' versus 'soft' measurement.
- Nomothetic (generalisable) or idiographic (unique to the individual) measures.
- Generic or specific measurement.
- Who does the measuring?
- Other design issues.

As you go through this chapter it may be helpful to think of a measure you are familiar with (perhaps one you have used) and consider how it fits into the broad map we are describing here. This will help you understand the issues.

'Hard' versus 'soft' measures

In engineering and the physical sciences, measurements can often be determined to very high reliability and with very high precision, but this is rarely the case in our field. Consider weight: in physical science, the same object weighed by different precision scales will show that weight to many decimal places and it will not change unless things are attached to it or shaved off it, nor will it change depending who puts the object on the scales. By contrast, feelings and psychological states, for example happiness, misery or coping, are just not measurable in the same way and will have different meanings for different individuals, differences that can be very important in measuring change and outcomes. This is essentially the distinction between 'hard' and 'soft' measurement.

'Hard measurement' refers to measurement systems external to the thing being measured; by contrast, 'soft' measures are mediated by an individual's own report and individual construction of the issue being measured. 'Hard' measures are often treated as if they are not open to interpretation whereas 'soft' measures are treated as if they are less robust or valuable by virtue of the interpretation involved in their creation and use.

There *are* 'hard' physical science measurements that are pertinent to therapies. The duration and frequency of sessions and lengths of therapies are crucial hard measures.

Biological measures and markers

There is a long tradition of 'hard' measures of stress: skin resistance/conductance (via sweating), heart rate, heart rate variability and respiratory rate. There is some resurgence of interest in these measures as computerised methods of analysing such data have developed. Currently, these are more likely to be used as therapy process markers rather than as change/outcome measures: for example, changes in client (or therapist) heart rate can be used to mark different phases within a session and may link to what is being discussed. However, these measures may move more into the outcome arena as their measurement becomes easier: evidence of stress diminishing over time might be a pertinent OM for some clients.

Blood chemistry measurements are paradigmatic hard measures and over the last 40 years interest in blood stress hormones, particularly cortisol, has waxed and waned. Again, it never became an OM although it is now of interest in relation to parent–infant transmission of stress and possible impacts on the carer-baby relationship. For the particular group of diabetic clients struggling with unstable blood control, HbA1c level, a marker of diabetic control, has obvious value as an outcome measure. As so often with these hard/soft and biology/mind distinctions, each can impact on the other: the psychological impacts of improved diabetic control can be huge and therapy here can create positive feedbacks with steadier and safer blood glucose levels, leading someone to feel less ill, and hence psychologically stronger. Therapy can promote such 'virtuous cycles' of change that can be demonstrated with both 'hard' and 'soft' measures.

'Brain activity' is another paradigmatic hard measure and the same 40-year period has seen an explosion in our ways of observing it. Before 1980, the only widely available tool was the electroencephalogram (EEG): a way of looking at electrical activity through the skull by placing a network of electrodes on the scalp. Since then, the ability to explore events inside the brain has changed dramatically with positron emission tomography (PET scanning) and magnetic resonance imaging (MRI). Functional MRI (fMRI) makes use of the fact that MRI can pick up events lasting a short time (a second or so). For example, if someone looks repeatedly at faces showing different emotions, fMRI signals can locate what parts of the brain are active in relation to observing particular emotions. Again, these tools may be able to show changes following therapy, but the costs and time involved mean that these will only ever be OMs for highly funded research projects, not routine OMs. To date, they seem only to have been used for a limited range of therapies: relaxation, meditation and mindfulness and behavioural activation interventions.

As ever, this touches on money and politics. The equipment is so expensive that if a hospital or university has invested in a hugely expensive scanner there is a pressure for the scanner to be fully used to justify the expenditure. This makes research with the machine the province of teams who have already used these tools and delivered results on time and to budget. Politically, leaders in these areas have significant sway with funding bodies about what to research, and the narrow range of therapies studied with these methods probably reflects this. It would be interesting to see large therapy organisations building collaborative links with these researchers as we believe that successful therapies do change brains.

A more serious political issue is the almost universal misperception that 'hard' measures, and particularly brain or biological measures, will produce more meaningful, longer lasting and more certain answers than 'soft' measures. This view continues despite the history that such waves of enthusiasm for hard measures rarely last and have yet to impact on routine therapies at all. The seductiveness of these 'hard' measures and perhaps an over-valued belief in their importance is a challenge for our field.

The simple polarisation of 'hard' versus 'soft' is in fact misleading as even apparently 'hard' measures may be subjective. For instance, a person's weight is a hard measurement: the scales are external to the individual and, with some sensible precautions, the person weighed cannot change what the scales say at any point in time and the measurement can be done with great precision. However, the psychological meaning of the weight may be highly personal. For a client with eating problems, even a weight so low that they are nearing renal failure may feel too high. More generally, age is a 'hard' measure, but one 40 year-old may feel fairly young, while another may be panicking about ageing; one 14 year-old may be full of post-pubertal desire and uncertainties, while another may be anxious at not yet having reached puberty. Despite these overlaps, which in our field mean that many hard measures take on softer and more complex dimensions, the distinction between hard and soft measures can be useful provided that it is not used to over-simplify things.

Nomothetic versus idiographic descriptors

Nomothetic descriptors relate to things that can be generalised or categorised and on which it is assumed everyone has a score. By contrast, idiographic descriptors are specific and can be unique to an individual. Height and weight are typical examples of nomothetic descriptors: no living person has ever had no height or no weight. By contrast, fingerprints or passport photographs are idiographic descriptors: everyone has fingerprints and can have a passport photograph but neither converts to a simple score. Idiographic descriptors give a picture ('graphic') unique to the individual ('idio').

Box 2.1 Key Terms

Idiographic: An idiographic measure gives a picture ('graphic') unique to the individual ('idio'). For example, a self-characterisation narrative written by a client will be a unique picture of how they see themselves.

Nomothetic: Nomothetic comes from the Greek for 'law'. It refers to things that are general to all, things that may operate according to certain rules: for example, measures on which it is assumed everyone has a score. Height and weight are paradigmatic examples. In talking therapies, the more common ratings may be for an imperfect but useful indication of 'depression' or 'risk' or 'well-being'.

Idiographic measures in psychological therapies might include a self-characterisation narrative written by a client, which will be a unique picture of how the client sees themselves. More quantitative idiographic measures include the Repertory Grid and card sort self-description methods. These idiographic measures are rich but it takes significant time for the client to complete a repertory grid or write a self-characterisation and further time is required to interpret them or create scoring protocols. However, 'personal questionnaires' and 'client generated measures' can be short enough to be usable as ROMs. A good example is PSYCHLOPS, which we will return to in Chapter 4.

In therapies, the nomothetic/idiographic distinction is not quite as clear as in those 'hard measurement' examples. You may be detecting a theme here about our field: binary distinctions are rarely as clear as they seem! For example, we use measures of 'well-being', 'quality of life', 'risk' or 'depression' as if each of those is a nomothetic dimension on which we each have a value which can be compared to someone else's. This idea is often based on asking people the same questions with the same range of scoring options. Going back to our theme around 'soft' versus 'hard', these scores are often disparaged as 'soft' for three main reasons:

1. The absence of gold standard measures.
2. Subjectivity: the fact that in both observer ratings and self-ratings different people may understand the measure differently.

3. Dimensionality: because, unlike a physical dimension like height in metres, such scales are not clearly unidimensional.

The first two issues, the lack of a gold standard, like the international definitions of a metre or a kilogram, and subjectivity in ratings, are self-explanatory, but this issue of dimensionality is worth unpacking. The simple beauty of measurements like height is that they need only one indicator: your height is your height, more or less accurately measured. This is the same for your weight: the measurement is unidimensional. By contrast, a map is two-dimensional, and an architectural scale model is three-dimensional. Equally, whether you are depressed involves a number of issues which are quite varied and can include suicidal thoughts, negative affects, cognitive distortions or physiological variables. This is not simply one-dimensional, it is multi-dimensional. Similarly, quality of life, risk and well-being are not simply one-dimensional.

Global, general/generic and specific measures

Linking with dimensionality, OMs can be global: trying to cover the entire realm of change in therapy; general/generic: trying to cover at least a broad domain; or specific: more nearly unidimensional. Examples of global measures include measures of quality of life or well-being, whereas specific measures might be of panic attacks or body weight concerns.

Specific change measures can be quite individually focused. For example, behaviour therapists might ask clients to rate specific behaviours: compulsive hand washing; level of anxiety felt in relation to a phobia. Such highly focused ratings may be idiographic, addressing a uniquely personal obsessional thought. Traditionally, these were therapist-generated measures used to rate change over the course of the treatment. This tradition of highly focused measurement in behavioural and some cognitive behavioural therapies has meant that some therapists in these modalities have been reluctant to use more general measures.

However, in many therapies, and we believe for many clients, the focus is broader - they may wish to feel better in a more general way, hence 'well-being' is a common general measure. Equally, a client may have a specific problem they want to change but that problem has a very general impact on how they function and feel. This is true even within a diagnostic framework in which problems are mapped to psychiatric/psychological diagnoses and a good outcome is seen as having been achieved when the client no longer meets criteria for the diagnosis. For example, 'depression', in all its many forms, impacts on relationships and these impacts may be as important, or more important, than 'the depression' to the client.

Moving away from diagnoses, other specific foci include: self-esteem, self-confidence, sociability, functioning in relationships, etc. For many counsellors and psychotherapists, such foci feel more congruent with their theory than diagnostically focused measures. Although measures of these foci may be nomothetic, they may be worded more in terms of feelings and relationships and may feel more personal and less 'pigeon-holing' than diagnostically focused measures.

It is also important to recognise that how measures are used varies across countries and the professions using them. In the UK, there is little tradition of diagnoses being made by measures. Perhaps this is linked with professional differences and diagnoses being seen as the work of psychiatrists, and many psychologists and therapists having some opposition to the reductionism or labelling that can go with diagnoses. By contrast, in mainland Europe, measures are often expected to be used to 'confirm' diagnoses or contribute to a 'diagnostic formulation', and measures that do not aspire to do this can be met with some puzzlement.

Through the start of the 21st century, therapy OMs have shifted from specific to more general measures. Typically, these have been shorter than 20th-century measures, short enough for routine use. The CORE-OM (CORE and CORE System Trust 2021) and the OQ-45 (OQ Measures, 2021) and their shortened versions are examples of such measures. Where clients have very specific problems, such as compulsions, phobias and eating disorders, general measures may need to be complemented by specific measures.

Who does the measuring?

This is a fundamental to OM and there are two main answers:

1. Someone else is rating the client: observer rating.
2. The client is rating themselves: self-rating methods.

Observer rating

Humans are a social species: instinctive raters of others. 'Observer ratings' are a basic and normal human activity: we all rate each other and ourselves much of the time. When we observe things that we like or find difficult in others, when we look up to or feel sympathetic to someone else, these experiences form an appraisal. These appraisals are a synthesis of historical experience and current observation. Observer-rated OM structures this innate process to focus on specific areas of experience and activity but the structuring is crucial.

Trained researcher ratings

Observer ratings have been among the dominant OMs in psychiatry and research psychology.

A classic example arising out of a diagnostic, psychiatric framework is the Hamilton Rating Scale for Depression (HRSD), which is a highly structured interview with a clear coding and scoring system. Nearer to the culture of psychological therapies is the Camberwell Family Interview (CFI), which includes ratings of Criticism, Emotional Over-involvement and Warmth based on observation in an interview with a family. A final example is rating of 'attachment' within the influential area of attachment theory. The Strange Situation Test (SST) is the original rating of child attachment and the Adult Attachment Interview (AAI) is a rating system based on a semi-structured interview with adults.

Most observer rating systems recommend, or stipulate, substantial training in order to seek consistency in the interview or process and in the rating of the observations. This consistency across raters is called inter-rater agreement and will be discussed more below and in Chapter 3. The time involved in training and carrying out the ratings make most of these rating systems impractical outside well-funded research.

Lay raters

Ratings by lay people form a key part of OM in child therapies where ratings by parents or carers/guardians are crucial. The parent version of the Strengths and Difficulties Questionnaire (SDQ), a rating of children's and young people's behaviours and emotions, is one of the most well-known and is widely used as a therapy OM.

Professionals and therapists as raters

Another set of measures involve ratings done by professionals engaged with the client. These lie between researcher ratings and lay ratings and usually involve little or no training beyond a rating handbook. Rating scales designed to be used by therapists to rate clients' states exist but it is perhaps interesting that none seem to have achieved wide use. More common ratings by professionals include ratings by teachers of pupils' behaviours in school and ratings of behaviour and social interaction designed to be completed by nurses and other professionals working in mental health and learning difficulty services.

Automated/computerised ratings

Most observational measures use humans to do the ratings, but it is worth noting that computer ratings are emerging. One such rating used in therapies involves computer processing of video recordings of sessions which give automatic ratings of the amounts of movement of the protagonists and can be used to explore how much protagonists' movements mirror each other. Similarly, processing of audio recordings can identify who is speaking and can detect rhythms, turn taking, over-talking, as well as using filtering to detect tonality. Perhaps reassuringly, to date such measures seem restricted to therapy process measurements rather than being used as OMs.

Self-ratings

By contrast with these various observer ratings, self-report ratings are currently much the most prevalent way of measuring therapy outcomes. Even in research settings where there are resources for using other rating methods, such as use of trained raters or 'hard' biological measures, self-report almost completely dominates. Self-report measures have huge strengths but also some limitations which are important to understand.

Strengths of self-rating

One strength of self-rating is cost. Provided that clients can meaningfully complete questionnaires about themselves, this is much cheaper than any other alternatives, even taking into account that some self-rating measures may be copyright and subject to reproduction fees.

Questionnaires can be completed by post, email, web forms or, increasingly, in phone apps. The data from them are very compact, standardised, easy to store and fairly easy to analyse. Quantitative questionnaire data can usually guarantee anonymity if sensible precautions are taken with identifiers and ID codes.

As self-report questionnaires have become almost ubiquitous in high and middle income countries, clients will understand what is involved in completing questionnaires. Similarly, as particular questionnaires are widely used, practitioners are becoming familiar with looking at clients' responses and scores. This also means that summary data from others' use of the same questionnaire may be easily understood and available for comparison.

Ironically, in these strengths also lie some disadvantages. The wide usage and general dominance of particular OM questionnaires can lead to the mistaken idea that they are the best for all of our clients. It is also easy to assume that typical multi-item self-report questionnaires are the only forms of self-rating when there are many other methods, including client-generated measures, personal questionnaires, self-characterisation narratives or drawings, card sorts, forced choice measures and repertory grids, any of which may be more suitable than multi-item questionnaire for particular clients or groups.

Coming back to the issue of the rater: one obvious strength of self-rating is that the rating is by the expert on the topic. If you believe, as we do, that the client should be at the heart of what drives the therapy, then this is both a methodological and a political strength as it highlights the user perspective. On the face of it, this also removes the inter-rater agreement challenge mentioned above: there is only one rater and surely theirs is the authoritative, gold standard, rating. However, it is not quite as simple as this. When questionnaires are well designed and focus on specific issues, the classical form of a self-rating questionnaire minimises the scope for different interpretations of the questions and thereby allows comparison between individuals. As with multiple raters, having multiple items/questions aims to minimise individual differences in interpretation. However, we can never know for certain that one person's interpretation of a question is the same as another's.

Limitations of self-rating – Conscious awareness

This idea that in self-rating *the* expert is doing the rating is in many ways true and is a great strength of such measures. However, these ratings rely on the person using their conscious awareness to make a judgement about themselves. It is not only analytic/dynamic therapies that believe there are limits to our immediate self-awareness. Behavioural therapies aim to change behaviour patterns and do not assume that the patterns are driven by conscious decisions; family therapies assume that things happen in families in patterns that no one can explain and that no one drives consciously; interpersonal and experiential therapies assume that there are aspects of the self that are central to change in therapy that are not amenable to the client to change deliberately. In all these theories an observer rating might offer something over and above self-ratings, so we should be careful about giving self-rating automatic gold standard status.

Design effects in creating questionnaires

The overarching question of this section – 'who does the measuring?' – also has implications for 'who writes the measures?' Questionnaires are designed by humans. Traditionally, they were designed by researchers and then by researcher/clinicians. In the last 20 years there has been a welcome increase in 'user involvement' in the design of newer measures. However, unless they are idiographic measures, they must be made of items answerable by most clients. It would be naïve to believe that the involvement of users completely prevents normative assumptions or items that can have different interpretations. Constructing questions that cover the full range of social/interpersonal issues is particularly hard. For example, items cannot be chosen which assume someone has a job, has an intimate partner or has a family. Going further, they cannot assume that it is inevitably a good outcome to have these things – despite the fact that these are common social assumptions. The detailed work of questionnaire design can be challenging. We will come back to this in Chapter 3, but it is important to consider these issues when thinking about OMs.

Other factors to consider in the design of outcome measures

We think you will now be aware that responses to items in rating scales or self-report questionnaires are rarely as simple as they might seem. In this section we want to set out a few of the complexities to bear in mind.

Types of ratings

There are many different ways to set out a scale for an item to be rated. The method chosen should take account of the question being asked, the use to be made of the data and crucially, the groups doing the answering. There are choices to be made in designing response formats. For example, a scale may have simple binary responses – 'yes' versus 'no' or 'happened today' versus 'did not happen today' – or they may have more than two response levels. For example, the CORE-LD measures for self-rating by individuals with learning difficulties have three – 'not at all', 'sometimes' or 'a lot' – whereas the standard CORE-OM for general usage with adults has five – 'not at all', 'only occasionally', 'sometimes', 'often' and 'most or all the time'. A rating scale might ask for a mark on a 10 cm-long line between 'Deeply suicidal today' and 'Very happy today'. This kind of scale is called a Visual Analogue Scale and can be measured to the nearest millimetre to create a 0–100 scale, although that level of precision is almost certainly too detailed to be meaningful. Generally, a balanced response spread is wise. For example,

Very dissatisfied < > dissatisfied < > neutral < >satisfied < > very satisfied

is balanced, whereas

Very dissatisfied < > neutral < > a little satisfied < > very satisfied < > Totally satisfied

is clearly weighted towards a more positive expectation.

Number of ratings

As noted, multi-item rating measures have come to dominate both observer and self-rating. These measures ask multiple questions about the issue in question. Inevitably, there is a trade-off between accumulating more information and the amount of time taken to complete the measure. A larger number of items will give better coverage of the issue to be rated and more distinctions in scores, but it will increase the amount of time needed to complete the rating and may cause boredom and carelessness in ratings or more missed answers in self-rating measures.

Time frames

When designing or choosing a measure, the time frame the respondent is asked to consider is important. Asking someone to consider the last 24 hours is very different from asking about the last month or about the whole of someone's life. The time frame must be appropriate to the focus and to the use to be made of the data. A 24-hour time frame might be important for suicidal feelings, one week to levels of anxiety and the lifetime focus fits experiences of trauma or bereavement.

In a different way, how frequently a measure will be used will also make a difference to its construction. Someone self-rating every day for a week generates different information from someone rating every session or just at the beginning and end of a therapy.

How much data do we have from different viewpoints?

Multiple raters

Having multiple raters brings two strengths and some challenges which we discuss below. The first strength is multiple raters may see different things and increase coverage. This is particularly important for global or generic ratings where one observer may know or see something another doesn't and will add validity. The second strength is that having multiple raters can cancel out randomness in ratings and increase reliability.

Common situations where at least some people are rated by more than one rater include multiple people rating an individual child (parent/carer, teachers, etc.) or multiple staff in an in-patient unit rating the same clients. Having multiple raters should give a more complete picture, increasing validity, as noted above: parents may see things that teachers cannot, and vice versa; their viewpoints may be complementary. Equally, random inter-rater rating differences will tend to cancel out while agreement between them will add up so that systematic signal can emerge. Where there are multiple raters rating the same people, statistical procedures allow us to explore inter-rater disagreement, for example that one rater may tend to rate more positively than another.

Frames of reference – differences in interpretation

Although a well-constructed questionnaire will try to minimise individual differences in interpreting particular items, people always bring their own frames of reference to the task and their interpretations of items may vary considerably. For example, if an item says 'I have felt warmth or affection for someone', how people understand 'warmth or affection' will differ to some extent between individuals. A person who has not had much warmth or affection in their life may answer 'sometimes' if they regularly chat to the person in their local corner shop.

This xkcd cartoon gives another great example:

Figure 2.1 xkcd cartoon: pain rating

Reproduced by kind permission of xkcd.com

So, comparability of responses between individuals is not automatic even with well-written nomothetic self-report instruments. Sometimes therapy allows people to take more seriously the difficulties they have experienced or offers insight into problematic patterns of relating that the person had not been aware of before. Such changes may affect them so they self-rate as less happy and well-functioning than they did earlier, even when practitioners and observers working with them would agree that they had made progress and were functioning better than they had been. We think this is a phenomenon often seen in forensic settings or with particularly emotionally deprived clients, although we have not seen empirical evidence exploring this: it is an area ripe for investigation.

A related issue is that when 'healthy' volunteers are given a self-rating measure of distress or dysfunction on two separate occasions, the mean score tends to be slightly less disturbed on the second occasion. The effect is small but fairly robust. Again, it may be that for at least some people the very act of completing a questionnaire changes their frame of reference a little.

Another important issue is that people may (deliberately or not) alter their answers depending on the use to which they imagine their answers will be put. We worry that the more political pressure is put on ROM data the more possible it will be that clients will rate their problems high at assessment, suspecting that this will make it more likely that they will be offered therapy. Similarly, at the end of therapy they may rate themselves higher in disturbance, hoping that this will prolong the work or to express anger that it is finishing, or else they may rate lower than they feel to 'thank' their therapist or in the hope that it will help support the service. Again, we know of no empirical evidence for these effects, but we find it odd that there seems to have been so little attempt to examine these possibilities.

Summary

In this chapter, we have tried to set out a broad framework of issues to be aware of when thinking about 'outcome' measures and 'outcome' measurement. It has touched on the nature of the measure (hard or soft); whether the measure is unique to the individual (fingerprints) or something most people have a value for (height); whether the thing being measured is general or specific (well-being or suicidality); the question of who does the measuring (the person themselves or an 'observer'); and finally, a range of other important factors to be aware of when thinking about what a measure is for. If you had in mind a measure you have used as you went through the chapter, we hope it helped you to see why thinking about these issues is important. How to make choices between measures will be looked at in detail in Part III when we talk about using measures in practice, but first we need to look at how you judge the quality of a measure, what measures are out there, and what you can do with the information that is collected. These questions form the basis of the next three chapters.

3

How to judge the quality of an outcome measure

Introduction

In Chapter 2 we gave you a general framework for thinking about outcome measures (OMs). In this chapter we aim to provide the basic information you need to be able to judge how good a measure is – its structure and whether it is fit for *your* purpose. The structural issues include general construction (readability, length, etc.) as well as psychometric properties (reliability, validity, etc.), but other important dimensions that are often neglected include practical matters like cost, whether the instrument is available in translation, whether other services use it or will start to use it if you do, etc. We will use the acronym 'GULP':

Generalisability

Usability

Linguistics and Cultural Location

Psychometrics

When we come to **P**sychometrics our focus is on multi-item, self-report questionnaire measures, although for the other areas we cover – the **GUL** headings – what we say applies to all measures.

But first a note of caution: our key theme throughout this book is about finding the balance between over-valuing and under-valuing OMs. OMs are often over-valued and equated with 'hard' measures in the physical sciences (Chapter 2) and then treated as if the findings are definitive in ways that go beyond the actual (and valuable) information they do convey (Chapter 10). Paradoxically, from a different stance, they are as often under-valued when equated with 'hard' physical sciences as they are seen as antithetical to the art of therapy. Both over- or under-valuation can be very unhelpful when trying to decide what to use and when: we need sensible valuations! There *are* good measures and bad measures but there are no perfect measures.

Philosophically, whether we are in the realm of physical or psychological 'science' the reality is that we are using measurement in human systems and we need to be attentive to the personal impact of what we use and when we use it. This xkcd cartoon brings this home poignantly as it follows the author's partner's cancer diagnosis. Numbers have implications and emotional impact.

Figure 3.1 xkcd cartoon: probability

Reproduced by kind permission of xkcd.com

So, having reminded ourselves that we are interested in using measures because they have real-life applications and powerful intra- and inter-personal meanings, let us look at the detail.

Generalisability, Usability, Linguistics and Cultural Location, and Psychometrics

GULP: Generalisability

Evaluation of a measure should always start with the content, with an idea of what you want from it, and with a target group with whom you want to use it. You also need to think about *how useful any findings you get from it will be to others*. This last bit is the crucial issue of generalisability and it relates to both your own aims and those for defined other settings. Nothing is useful unless it is suitable for your specific aims; at the same time, no OM generalises to be useful for everything.

Content and response systems

The question 'How are you today?' starts a measurement. In fact, 'How are you?' and 'How have you been...?' are the root of all therapy change measures but some practitioners will ask them a lot, and some will try never to ask such direct questions. Until you add '...on a scale from 0 to 10 where 0 is ... (e.g. very bad) and 10 is ... (e.g. great)', the response is going to be of very localised meaning, probably localised to that one client. However, if you are disciplined about using the same phrasing every time, across different sessions and different clients, then you gain comparability across different clients: you start to get generalisability.

This is a simple example, but conventional OMs take this principle and refine and extend it (and relieve you from imposing such repetitive language on your conversations with clients). The first step is to put questions on paper, or a screen, removing variation between different therapists in tone of voice, facial expression, etc. Multi-item questionnaire OMs also extend things by offering a range of responses (the response system) and by asking a number of different questions:

> 'Over the last week: I have felt terribly alone and isolated.'
>
> 'Over the last week: I have felt OK about myself.'
>
> 'Over the last week: my problems have been impossible to put aside.'

By doing this, the underlying issue of interest is addressed in different ways. As already noted in Chapter 2, response options will be fixed: they may be a simple 'yes'/'no' or they may grade intensity, 'very much so' to 'hardly at all', or grade fit, 'absolutely agree' to 'does not apply to me at all', or grade frequency, 'all the time' to 'never'.

Here are some key questions to ask about any measure. It is not an exhaustive list, but it covers the main areas:

- Do the items make sense to you and address things that matter to you?
- Will they make sense to your clients?
- What do they not cover? Is there anything vital for your purposes that is missing? Bear in mind that no measure can cover everything and some issues that can be explored in a conversation simply cannot be reduced to usable written questions.
- Does the response system make sense and fit the question that precedes it? Will it be comprehensible for your clients?
- Does the measure have a time frame (for example, the past week)? Is that time frame sensible for your purposes? It is rare that a measure does not need a time frame.

- What reading/learning level does the measure demand? Does it have complex clauses, double negatives, words some people might not know? Does it have words or phrases that seem quaint, dated or inappropriate? What impact will using it have on people?
- Does the introduction at the top of the measure seem likely to 'speak' to your target group, to encourage them to complete all the items as honestly as possible?
- Are any items hard to answer for some clients? For example, do they ask about a partner or a job? If so, they may not be usable with some people.
- What normative assumptions are made? Are those assumptions problematical either generally or for your particular topic of interest or your clients?
- Are the questions relative/comparative? For example, some questionnaires ask about change from a normal state and some explicitly say 'compared with others...'. Will this work for your clients?

As you go through this checklist, you will probably find that it is easy to criticise measures and you should also see that it is harder to construct really good measures/questionnaires than it might appear.

Audience

No measure is perfect for all therapists' interests nor for all clients. However, another issue you should consider is the audience with whom you might share your findings: measures vary in their persuasive power for different audiences. Some OMs are more persuasive for one profession than for another; some are more persuasive for one modality than another; some are more persuasive in one culture or country than another. We will come back to this below. Don't despair! Accept that no measure, not even the one you are now tempted to write, is perfect! We are back to navigating a path through this; seeking a measure that is good for your purposes, but recognising it will not be perfect, is the vital first step to good use of OMs.

Don't make changes to a measure!

If you are choosing from existing measures, you may be tempted to make a tweak to one that you think will improve it for your purposes, clients or audience. Don't do it! Most measures are copyright and, in fact, any original piece of work is copyright unless it explicitly says to the contrary. Remember, therefore, that even if an OM is free to reproduce, it is still copyright, making it illegal to change it. Even if a measure is explicitly free to use *and* to change, there is the generalisability issue: if you change a measure, even in quite minor ways, you will change how people complete it and scores will no longer be comparable with other people's scores. Just don't do it!

GULP: Usability

Before deciding to use a measure, think about some of the practical and logistical implications of using it and then do some field testing. Time always matters, so check how long it takes you and other people to complete it. In principle, the more time clients give you the more you can learn, but time is rarely freely available. If filling in measures takes a very long time (not unusual in research), you lose comparability with routine therapy practice. Both very short and very long time scales may set up particular expectancies for clients and these may affect how they respond. An ultra-brief measure can imply to the client that 'these seven questions are the only thing that matters'. Long measures that focus on the same theme and ask the same question in many similar but slightly different ways can suggest that the first response of the client is not deemed trustworthy. And very long measures can simply engender boredom, loss of concentration or frank irritation.

These acceptability issues also bear on how often you want clients to complete the measure. A measure that may be acceptable in length at the first meeting may be too long if repeated every session, but using a very short measure in order to have data every week may lose breadth of coverage. We think that mixing lengths of measures and repetition (e.g. longer pre and post, and shorter measures taken more frequently in between start and finish) is a neglected option. The key is to think about usability against what you want from the data, for your own setting.

Cost is also a factor that is sometimes overlooked. Long measures obviously have costs in terms of your clients' time, but there will also almost always be increased data processing costs with more time needed for data entry and analysis. Most people underestimate the time and the support needed to digest and analyse data, so being mindful of the costs downstream is vital. As well as time costs, there are direct financial costs for many copyright measures: many measures are not free and licences may make their use very costly. A reproduction charge of £2/2€/$2 per usage can be prohibitive if the measure is used frequently or in a large service.

GULP: Linguistics and Cultural Location

Attention to linguistic and cultural issues is vital if we are to compare data across borders and population groups. Until recently, Western ethnocentrism has dominated our field, but that is changing and there are rich gains to be had if ideas, practice and data are shared and differences are explored openly. Some measures can be translated and will work across these boundaries, but others may not. This may reveal some important differences in cultures and these may not be just linguistic. Take body image and obesity/anorexia. Weight for height is fairly easy to measure with good precision, but weight for height can mean very different things in different cultures.

When considering using a translation of a measure, beware of translations whose authors make bland assertions of comparability or assume that high reliability equates to a good translation (we will come back to reliability below, in the 'P' of GULP). A description of the translation methods and some discussion of possible limits of transferability should exist for any translation you use. Good protocols for translation stress the importance of using multiple independent translations and then field testing with qualitative exploration. This is different from the paradigm of 'forward-translation and independent back-translation' that was dominant for many years. In that approach, the measure is first translated into the target language and then a different translator translates the measure back into the original language blind to the original. This has obvious appeal: if the back-translation is clearly semantically equivalent to the original, we would appear to have cast-iron evidence that the translation is a good one. However, the problem is that language and meaning are not that simple. A classic example is the item 'I have had the feeling of butterflies in my stomach' in the Hospital and Anxiety Depression Scale (HADS) (Stern, 2014). This nice colloquial expression used in UK English for somatic anxiety causing palpitations and/or churning in the guts is widely used in the English-speaking world, and so it works well as an indicator of anxiety in that linguistic location. It is also easy to translate into another language: 'butterflies' and 'stomach' are not obscure words so the forward-translation goes fine as does the back-translation. However, if the phrase does not exist with that meaning in the target language, then the item will be meaningless to most of the target user group. This was exactly the situation found in one study of the Arabic HADS and was only recognised when psychometric field testing showed that the item was not working as it should. Simple qualitative field testing with a small number of people who spoke Arabic but not English would have detected the problem.

GULP: Psychometrics

Psychometrics embraces the logical, mathematical and statistical ideas that can help to evaluate the qualities of psychological measures. Maths and statistics are not commonly the comfort zone of therapists; equally, epistemology is not often the comfort zone of psychometricians. Despite this, there is much in psychometrics that is very helpful, although there is also much that is seriously oversold and totemised and psychometric analyses are often reified and treated as 'gold standard tests' in ways that make little sense.

Just as no questionnaire will ever be perfect, no psychometric tool should ever be thought of as definitive and persuasive to all audiences. What follows, we hope, will give you a sound and sensible grasp of the psychometric explorations that are commonly used and how they can help us to evaluate measures, particularly when used across substantial numbers of people.

Moving from epistemology to the psychometric exploration of measures

The terms we are going to look at here are ones referred to in research articles and journal papers and include the 'psychometric parameters' often used to judge traditional quantitative measures. As we have noted, multi-item scales have come to dominate OM and these are usually what is meant by 'quantitative research tools' in our field. Most of the remainder of this chapter will focus on them.

Until recently, almost every paper referring to the use of questionnaire measures will have a line that we parody as:

> Asterix's measure of gallic tendencies has established *reliability* (Cronbach's alpha .91; La Pierre et al., 1960a) and convergent *validity* with Greatorix's Inventory (GI; Stone et al., 1961), Pearson correlation .78 (Rock et al., 1965b).

We will discuss these key terms 'reliability' and 'validity' later; Cronbach's alpha and Pearson's correlation are names of two specific statistical indices. Such information *can* provide helpful markers as to whether a measure has worked well in a particular setting, and they tell us about how it worked for a particular set of people who completed the measure. However, we need to recognise that these numbers are not, contrary to the implication of that invented sentence above, fixed properties of our measures. Cultural differences and literacy differences can mean that the same measure can show very different psychometric results in different samples even if all participants completing it share the same first language and that is the language of the measure. Mispresenting psychometric properties as fixed for the measure in all settings is to equate our measures with physical science measures and damages real understanding of how OMs can help our field.

Reliability

Internal reliability

Reliability is about measuring something consistently. In psychometrics, reliability is the extent to which your measurement is signal as opposed to random noise. A perfect measure would be all signal and no noise and have a reliability of 1.0. That is impossible for therapy OMs but does help us to understand reliability. If an OM is made of items that have nothing in common, then a score based upon them will be entirely noise and have reliability of zero. A good measure will have items that reflect the underlying issue of interest, and the more the items reflect that issue of interest then the more the scores on the items across many people will inter-correlate and the higher the reliability of the measure.

So, a good multi-item measure contains separate items that are each imperfect reflections of an underlying thing you want to measure. You have imperfect measurement but the pooling of different items means that the signal can emerge from the noise. This is the central idea driving multi-item measurement and allows us to give a value for 'internal reliability' from the extent to which items are correlated positively. The most widely used summary statistic measuring internal reliability is Cronbach's alpha.

Test-retest reliability

Where a state or trait that interests us is fairly stable, we can also look at reliability in another way: by seeing to what extent scores at one point in time correlate with scores a time later. A high correlation supports the idea that the measure is reliable. The time between measurements is important: if we are measuring something presumed to be a personality trait, we may expect it to fluctuate relatively little and a test-retest interval in months may make sense. For a state issue like mood, we believe it *does* fluctuate over time so a shorter interval will be more appropriate – one week is a common choice. Simple correlations have to be interpreted sensibly. The stability of answers to questions that have little or nothing in common does not stop the sum of scores on the items being nonsense. As with internal reliability, we can see that perfect test-retest reliability is probably not a goal to be sought, but zero test-retest reliability says that we are either measuring something that changes very rapidly or there is something wrong with our measure.

Inter-rater reliability

Most therapy OMs draw on the view of just one person: the one filling in the measure, almost always the client. However, there is much to be gained when more than one person rates something, as noted in Chapter 2. Inter-rater reliability refers to the extent to which different raters agree when rating the same thing, for example the behaviour of children in class. When therapists and clients rate the client's change, it is actually quite unusual that the two viewpoints show very high agreement. That is not terribly surprising as, obviously, the two rating positions are very different and the frames of reference of clients and of therapists can be very different. However, we would hope that most clients and therapists will have some agreement.

In Chapter 2 we noted that where there are multiple ratings, random inter-rater variations will tend to cancel out, but agreement between them will add up so that a systematic signal can emerge. This assumes a degree of consistency or inter-rater reliability. However, there are occasions where one rater may be more extreme in their inconsistency and one reason for looking at inter-rater agreement is to be able to see when there is 'unreliability'. For example, if a member of staff rating clients' involvement in activities in an inpatient setting makes ratings more affected by their own mood state than the client's behaviour, this might produce inconsistencies relative to the other staff raters that will result in marked random effects (unreliability). If one staff member consistently rates higher than another, this would result in a systematic effect ('invalidity' or bias, see below). The details are beyond the scope of this book but there are good statistical methods to tease such things apart.

Validity

As well as 'reliability', the other magic word in psychometrics is 'validity'. A good way to explain this is in terms of archery: reliability is whether you can cluster your arrows in a particular place, and validity is how near that place is to the bullseye. As with reliability, in our field, no measurement is perfectly valid: where unreliability is made up of inevitable contamination of a measure by *random* noise, invalidity is made up of inevitable contamination by *systematic* influences from some other variables than the one we want to measure: bias.

No validity without reliability

This is a wise adage in measurement and in psychometrics: a measure showing no (near zero) internal reliability is not going to be a valid measure of anything.

Just as there are a number of aspects of reliability, there are a number of aspects of validity.

- Face validity

'Face validity' describes the extent to which something appears to measure what it is supposed to measure. A questionnaire that is meant to assess anxiety but only asks questions about relationships lacks face validity.

- Convergent validity

Sometimes a measure may be good enough to be deemed a 'gold standard' measure. One way to evaluate a new measure is to see how well it correlates with the gold standard measure. This is called *convergent validity*. Convergent validity might be between two measures of the same type, say between two self-rating questionnaire measures. However, convergent validity might also compare two measures of different types: for example, when scores on self-report measures correlate highly with ratings by observers. When you are creating the first ever measure of something, you do not have any measure against which to assess convergent validity. This is one of the many reasons to be very wary of creating a new measure.

One specific and rather counter-intuitive form of convergent validity in our field is the *difference* in scores where theory about what you are measuring says there *should* be a difference. This is testing convergence between data and theory. A key example for therapy OMs is score differences between 'clinical' samples and 'non-clinical' samples. Here we *expect* to find divergence in scores and this is a good test of the convergence of theory and data. In fact, this is a good and relatively simple test of any 'outcome measure'.

As ever though, our usual mantra applies: the process is not perfect and there will be a subset of people not in the 'clinical group' who may need help, or be receiving it but who choose not to tell you; equally, in the 'clinical' group there may be some people with problems that are not the problems that the measure covers, especially if the outcome measure is specific not general. Despite these caveats, one key convergent validity check for any therapy OM is the difference between scores in 'clinical' and 'non-clinical' groups, so much so that we should probably avoid measures that have not tested these differences.

- Divergent or discriminant validity

This is the complement to convergent validity. It refers to situations where there is no relationship between two constructs and hence you expect no correlation between the scores (divergence). For example, if you believed that age should have little correlation with well-being in the adult population, then finding a near zero correlation between scores on your measure and age in a large sample would be a reassuring example of 'divergent validity'. Of course, in many societies age is associated with psychological variables, so aspects of well-being will probably show statistically significant if small relationships with age. For example, older people may be lonelier and more challenged by health problems than younger people; equally, younger people may have more worries about identity and social functioning than older people. Age effects on psychological variables are rarely either absolutely non-existent or simple. Similarly, gender associations are also rarely things we can say *must* be zero.

Unfortunately, many psychological issues show correlations with each other and can sit in an uneasy area between convergent and divergent validity. For example, depression will correlate positively with anxiety, with (low) self-esteem and with (poor) social functioning. This could be seen as poor divergent validity and that measures of these issues were badly designed. However, it is also very possible that all the items on the measures are well chosen and the positive correlation reflects a real correlation between those dimensions: probably many people who are markedly anxious are also at least somewhat depressed.

- Predictive validity

Another important form of validation is whether whatever you measure predicts what it should. For example, does a measure of 'resilience' relate to how well people undergoing life events cope and retain well-being? This would take quite a large and carefully designed study but is feasible. Sadly, such tests are rarely conducted in our field, presumably because they are much more resource intensive than simple cross-sectional explorations of convergent and divergent validity.

From face validity to content validity

These empirical correlations and associations are all very well, but they sit on top of vital qualitative issues. As noted, face validity asks: 'Does the measure look to have items that tap the things we think *are* good reflections of the underlying construct we want to measure?' and 'Do they look as if they are fairly unlikely to be contaminated with other issues?'

Face validity is really the start of 'content validity'. However, content validity is also about trying to ensure that the measure has not omitted any key indicators of the issue in focus. Does a measure of, say, 'authenticity' cover most or all the aspects of the term in Carl Rogers' writings? How well does it cover post-Rogerian theories?

Where a measure has separate scales, content validity can be explored quantitatively, although this is surprisingly rarely reported. For example, some content validity for the HADS (Hospital Anxiety and Depression Scale) can be tested by asking people to put the 14 items in two piles, one anxiety related, one depression related, and seeing if the allocations fit with the scale design?

The HADS illustrates an important measure design issue: the designers wanted to measure anxiety and depression in people with physical illnesses (hence the 'Hospital' in the name). Because of this, they deliberately omitted aspects of anxiety and of depression that might be contaminated by consequences of physical illnesses, for example low energy can be a part of depression but is also linked to much physical illness. Here we can see that face and content validity are not just about the issue you want to measure, but are also about the target population with whom you want to use the measure.

- Construct validity

The definitions of construct validity have evolved and changed and it is often seen as encompassing all empirical, statistical exploration of validity. The crucial point here is 'statistical'. Determining face and content validity is generally done essentially qualitatively: do people agree that the measure appears to measure what it says it does (face validity) and do they agree that it covers enough of that issue and that it is not contaminated with items likely to be affected by other systematic variation? This is sometimes called 'concept mapping' a measure.

Construct validity is quantitative: it is a statistical exploration of the answers given by people completing the measure. For example, what do the item ratings tell you when you give the HADS to a lot of people? Do the anxiety items tend to correlate more highly with each other than with the depression items and do the depression items correlate more strongly with each other than with the anxiety items?

Factor analysis is a statistical methodology, which is widely reported in the literature, that addresses these questions. Factor analysis tests whether some items in a measure seem to have more in common (correlate strongly) across data samples than do other items. To this extent, if the seven anxiety items correlate highly and form one 'factor' in the sample data and the seven depression items form another, then the factor analysis has supported the construct validity of the HADS (broadly, this is what is found when the HADS is analysed). Factor analysis can, therefore, be a very useful way of exploring the apparent strength of a measure, but sadly it can also become a meaningless way to denigrate a measure which never claimed a particular structure.

This happens because there are measures whose design priority was coverage rather than possession of a nice factor structure. The CORE-OM is a clear example. Its 34 items were chosen to cover four domains: well-being, problems, functioning and risk. The items were chosen as earlier work suggested that these were domains that most therapists, regardless of modality, and most clients, across a diversity of problems, thought were targets for change in therapy. These were moderately semantically distinguishable domains but the designers never thought that people's distress split neatly into these as cleanly separable factors. It would be hard to have a sense of well-being while functioning poorly or suffering with many problems; in turn, suffering a lot of problems will impair social functioning, and vice versa. In the design phase of CORE-OM development, it was thought that risk, particularly risk to others, would be a rather distinct issue, less correlated with those content domains, but it was certainly not expected that these six items (touching both risk to self and to others – very different variables) would form a neat factor. A final feature was that the design involved using both positively cued items (e.g. 'I have felt OK') and negatively cued ones (e.g. 'I made plans to end my life'). This was done to avoid response bias and also to produce a measure that was not relentlessly negative and that would have broad coverage with relatively few items. There was good prior evidence that positive and negative feelings are not simply opposite ends of a spectrum but rather more complex (i.e. it is possible to have both positive and negative feelings at the same time and probably some of us are more likely to have such mixed feelings than others). The designers recognised that including positively keyed items would further complicate the identification of any simple factor structure, but as no such neat structure was expected, the inclusion of positively keyed items seemed wise and was supported in qualitative field testing.

Despite clearly showing that, as expected, the instrument did not have a neat factor structure in the first exploration of it and describing the reasons for that in real detail in a later paper, it has been fascinating to see how often the CORE-OM is criticised for not having a neat cross-sectional factor structure when it was designed with no intention of having this. There are many similar examples in the literature and the moral is to beware critiques that criticise measures and data for being something they ever claimed to be or needed to be!

Sensitivity to change

One final psychometric property is *sensitivity to change*. Clearly, how much scores change with therapy is not just a function of the sensitivity of the measure but also of how much real change there was over the period of the therapy. A good measure of change in therapies should have evidence that it can pick up improvement (or deterioration) in therapy and we advise against using any measure as a therapy OM if it has not shown such sensitivity. Interestingly, though correlating one off scores on one measure against scores on another is a commonly reported test of convergent validity, it is very rare that *change* on one OM across therapy is correlated with change on another as a convergent validity test.

Validity and audience

We have said that research and evidence are about communication to an audience. Different audiences are going to be both interested in and persuaded by different things. Understanding how psychometric tools address these different interests will help you to critique them constructively. To illustrate this, take depression measures. One of the most famous creators of the cognitive therapies, Aaron T. Beck, created a number of measures. The most successful, his Beck Depression Inventory (BDI) (Beck et al., 1961; Beck et al., 1988), has become, across two iterations (now the BDI-I and BDI-II), perhaps the most used of all self-report therapy OMs and a paradigm-defining measure. However, this was not independent of the work Beck and others were doing to create cognitive therapies, particularly for depression, and the BDI was specifically designed to be congruent with cognitive therapies and is perhaps particularly persuasive to cognitive therapists.

By contrast, another paradigmatic outcome measure, perhaps *the* paradigmatic observer rated outcome measure, the Hamilton Rating Scale for Depression (HRSD), was designed by a psychiatrist to fit a psychiatric understanding of depression, particularly for the psychiatric audience (Hamilton, 1960). That audience, although now increasingly willing to allow self-report measures into its journals, remains more oriented towards expert ratings based on entirely or heavily structured interview schedules. Although data from the HRSD has been subjected to factor analysis, psychiatrists' interest when the HRSD was first published was far more on inter-rater reliability, a good example that it is not only that different measures have different persuasive power to different audiences, but also that different psychometric tools have different importance for different audiences.

We do not think it is helpful for theoretical affiliations to become sectarian and for the choice of measure to limit audiences. However, thinking about the acceptability of your measure to your audience does matter, so be aware that different audiences put different value on different measures and on different psychometric explorations of those measures.

Shall I just invent my own measure? Stop! Don't do it! Don't jump!

Well, trying to create your own measure is not automatic methodological suicide, but it is generally very unwise to do this. We hope that if you have read this far in this chapter you can see that making up measures is not, to use an old cliché, rocket science, but the design of good measures is about dogged attention to face validity, to logistics and to readability. If that work is done well and what you want to measure is not rare or esoteric, then empirical psychometric exploration is the icing on the cake and will generally find usable parameters of reliability and validity.

However, although this is not rocket science, it is *very* easy to make bad measures and making good measures generally relies on a lot of experience. A new measure needs a number of checks on reliability, ideally in multiple samples. It also needs exploration for effects of possible sources of invalidity: gender, age, education, culture. At least some minimal testing of convergent and divergent validity is also needed. These are not trivial pieces of work and a measure that has not had these things explored in appropriate samples should not be used.

Another reason not to make your own measure is that a measure that has built a network of usage, and has become one that practitioners know, has a huge advantage over any new measure. Unless a new measure is radically better than an existing one it is unlikely to get used if there is a measure already in wide use. In the psychometric world, creating new measures where ones already exist tends to be an evolutionary blind alley.

For adult clients who are able to read questionnaires there are probably still some niche needs for new outcome/change measures (see Table 4.2 in Chapter 4), but generally there are already good enough measures for that client population. However, there are other client groups with real needs for better outcome and change measures: we almost certainly need more and better measures for children (as opposed to adolescents); for clients in forensic settings; and for people with more than mild learning difficulties. Finally, although there are many measures of personality, resilience and personality difficulties and/or personality disorder, these often tend to be 'McCarthy-ite' measures – 'Are you now or have you ever been...?' – which makes them very poor or useless as measures of change. Developing good measures of personality change through therapy will be challenging but is definitely needed.

If you do work in an area which is not well provided with existing measures, then, by all means, do start piloting new very simple measures. However, generating a definitive new one really is an expensive, multi-member team project if it is to be done well so you must have a substantial team of colleagues and collaborators with whom to do this and the funding to enable you to do the necessary work.

What about 'single study' measures?

Sometimes there is a clear logic for a simple questionnaire for a study, for example if researching a particular service for niche problems where no good existing measure fits what is needed. Where there is a case for a 'single study' measure our suggestions are:

1. Try to think through all the GULP issues we have defined above. Criticise your first ideas mercilessly.
2. Put it through iterative piloting with friends and colleagues using the GULP framework to get their feedback on it. Try to ask people with different literacy levels, specialists in the field and people completely outside the field. Try to ask some people whose first language is not that of the measure and people who have different cultural locations.
3. When you use it, if any of the above psychometric aspects, reliability and validity can be empirically explored, do build that into your first use of your tool.
4. Whatever you find when you use it:

    a. Make that publicly available, even if it is just in a summary or your thesis, or on a website so that you get Google scholar at least to index it. Ideally, include the findings in an indexed and publicly accessible journal paper.

b. Make the measure 'copyleft': if the measure is your original work, you automatically have the copyright on it and can charge other people for using it and it is illegal for them to take it and change it without your permission. That is true whether or not you put a '©' symbol on it, although it is best to do that. 'Copyleft' is not a legal term but covers many situations in which you keep your copyright but choose not to charge for reproduction. Good copyleft licences exist (e.g. https://creativecommons.org/) and make it clear whether you are allowing the construction of derivative measures or forbidding that. This will depend on how definitive and final you think your tool is. Using such licences also ensures that (honest) people using your tool will give attribution to you and this builds the network of knowledge about it.

Format

Throughout the 20th century, almost all therapy OM questionnaires were 'paper and pencil' measures. However, in the 21st century, OMs are increasingly delivered across the internet as interactive web pages or as 'apps' for phones and tablets. This has been accelerated by the shift to online therapies with the coronavirus pandemic of 2020. Delivering OMs in this way has the obvious advantages of cutting out transcription errors and of saving time. One important issue is that often delivering OMs this way can remove the option to omit items, so responses can be different from those from paper delivery of the same OM. Depending on the pressures, real or perceived, on clients to complete measures, this may lead to fewer non-completions but it may lead to more complete refusals to complete the measure. This also removes 'pro-rating', where a score is computed despite some missing items by taking the mean score of the items that were completed.

Different measures have different rules about the proportion of missing items that can be pro-rated, for example the CORE rule is that up to 10% of missing items can be pro-rated, so up to three items may be omitted or not scorable on the 34-item CORE-OM and a total score still computed. Where items differ considerably in their 'tuning' (e.g. 'I made plans to end my life' versus 'I have felt unhappy'), removing pro-rating can change score distributions, particularly on measures which may allow pro-rating of a high proportion of missed items. In principle, changing the format of a measure and removing pro-rating should only have small effects on scores, but it will be good to see empirical explorations of this.

The other main effect of format is that clients may respond to a questionnaire differently if they perceive it as more directly 'going into a machine'. It has been argued, with some empirical evidence, particularly for measures addressing issues of which people may be ashamed, that completion of measures directly to computer with little or no human interaction involved may lead to more honest and complete disclosure.

Summary

In this chapter we summarised how to judge the quality of OMs with our acronym GULP: generalisability, usability, language and cultural location, and psychometrics. We took you into the two main parts of psychometric evaluation: reliability and validity. We hope we have persuaded you not to invent your own measure and we have briefly explored elements of what happens as measures increasingly move from 'paper and pencil' to direct electronic completion.

4

An overview of outcome and change measures

In this chapter we will give an introduction to different categories of outcome and change measures, exploring some of the issues about modality, client group and client problem area. We then discuss a few measures in detail to explore issues when selecting a measure. This chapter is not a compendium or general guide but builds on the earlier more theoretical chapters to give a concrete framework for therapists wanting to use and choose appropriate routine change measures. We have listed a number of commonly used measures in tables, where we have focused mainly on measures that are free to use as we believe most therapists will not be able to afford measures with significant reproduction charges. That we mention a specific measure means we believe it has sufficient strengths for ROM in at least some therapies and some circumstances, but not that it is better than competitors. Equally, that a measure is not here does not indicate that we feel it is a bad measure. The categories that we will discuss, with examples, are the following:

- Modality specific measures
- Measures by client group
- Measures by focus e.g. 'problem area'
- Quality of Life and Proxy measures

We will finish with some key practicalities when using measures.

Declaration of interests

Chris has been involved in the development of the CORE-OM and LD-CORE and, to a lesser extent, the SCORE, YP-CORE and shortened forms of the CORE-OM, and he has led all but one of the approved translations of the CORE-OM and YP-CORE. He has also been involved in developments of PSYCHLOPS and the BSQ (Body Shape Questionnaire). This influenced the inclusion of all these measures, but all are free to use so the influence is not monetary.

Four measures, the PHQ-9, GAD-7, IAPT phobia scales and the WSAS (Work and Social Adjustment Scale), form the mandatory minimum self-rating information to be collected from clients at all contacts within the English NHS (National Health Service) IAPT (Improving Access to Psychological Therapies) services. As these are free to use and extremely widely used in the UK, we also mention them here. We drew on two UK Department of Health sponsored resources: the 2008 compendium of measures for adult mental health issues (https://www.rcpsych.ac.uk/docs/default-source/members/divisions/scotland/faculties/scotland-faculties-addictions-national-institute-for-mental-health-in-england-outcomes-compendium.pdf?sfvrsn=963d872e_2) and the CORC (Child Outcomes Research Consortium) list of 'Outcome and Experience Measures' for use with children and adolescents (Child Outcomes Research Consortium, 2021). We also recommend looking at the NHS National Clinical Content Repository (NHS Digital, 2021), which is a resource that has information about copyrights and legal issues in using scales, particularly the IAPT therapies dataset.

As will be clear from the earlier chapters, there are no perfect measures and no measure is optimal for all uses.

Categories of measures

Measures aligned with therapy modalities

We understand the wish to have modality specific change measures and noted in Chapter 3 that some widely used OMs were developed for specific modalities of therapy. However, this does not make them irrelevant for other therapeutic modalities as they often have broad elements that are common to most clients' experiences. Having said this, there is one modality which may make a specific OM necessary: in family/systemic work where the focus is on the health and functioning of the system not that of any one member, then it is clearly necessary to have measures to rate the family, although that does not preclude also asking each family member about themselves with a general measure or one from another modality. Modality specific measures inevitably prioritise professionals' views over clients' views as modalities are developed within professional networks.

Table 4.1 gives some examples of measures located in particular modalities and some generic/pantheoretical measures.

Table 4.1 Measures by modality or model of change

Model	**Measure**	**Comments/notes**
Diagnostically focused/ psychiatric	PHQ-9	IAPT required measures. Discussed in the text
	GAD-7	
	SCL-90R	Not free, long, multiple scales
	SCL-90	Thought to be free precursor of SCL-90R
	HADS	Not free, two scales for anxiety and depression
Cognitive	BDI-I & BDI-II	All arose from Beck's key work developing CBT, not free
	BAI	
	Hopelessness scale	
	Dysfunctional thoughts questionnaire	
Psychodynamic/ analytic	Depressive Experiences Questionnaire	
	Defense Style Questionnaire	
	Quality of Object Relations	
	Attachment Measures	The Adult Attachment Interview was not designed as an outcome measure and there are problems using it as one. Attachment related questionnaires have ratings that do not correlate well and should be used cautiously.
	SWAP	A therapist rated measure of personality
Interpersonal/ humanistic	Meaning in Life	
	Authenticity Scale	
Family/systemic	SCORE-15	
Generic/ pantheoretical	CORE	Free, various lengths, discussed more in case example in text
	GHQ	Not free, various lengths
	OQ	Not free, various scales, USA based
	Compass	Not free, various scales, USA based
	WSAS	Work and Social Adjustment Scale. With PHQ-9 and GAD-7, a mandatory part of the IAPT minimum data set.
	ReQoL	Quality of life measures tuned to MH QoL issues, see notes on QoL measures in the text
Client-generated and hybrid measures (see notes in text)	PSYCHLOPS	Very short hybrid measure
	Personal Questionnaire	Longer pure client-generated measure

Measures aligned with particular client groups

There are many possible ways to categorise client groups but Table 4.2 gives one simple breakdown including some often-overlooked groups with particular needs.

Table 4.2 Measures by client group

Client group	**Measure**	**Comments/notes**
Adults in general	All from Table 4.1	See in text and examples below
Adults with low literacy	Currently none known to us	
Deaf adults	British Sign Language versions of the CORE-OM, PHQ-9 and GAD-7	See in text and translations
Blind adults	Braille and audio versions of measures but these are uncommon	See in text
Adolescents	YP-CORE	Free, part of CORE system, see in text
	Y-OQ	Not free, part of OQ system
	SDQ	Free, versions for child, parents/carers and school staff
	RCADS	Free, self-report
Mild to moderate learning difficulties/ disability	LD-CORE-14 and LD-CORE-30	Free, part of CORE system
	Glasgow Anxiety and Depression scales	
Children	CORS	

It should be noted that people with acquired cognitive impairments (brain trauma, dementias, etc.) may have specific difficulties with comprehension so that self-report measures may be unsuitable and unhelpful for this group. Clearly there are also issues for adults with low or no literacy and we are not aware of any measures for this group, although the potential for the development of measures with pictograms or items to be read aloud seems clear.

That raises another issue: the language of the measure. As noted in Chapter 3, translating self-report measures, particularly those suitable for use as therapy OMs, is not a trivial process and we would recommend very strongly that people do not use translations that have not documented their translation process and shown that the process was thorough and culturally appropriate. Even when a translation has been done well, it is extremely unlikely that the psychometric properties of the translation will be the same as in another language so psychometric parameters from meaningful samples in the target language should be sought if comparative use is to be made of the data.

One scenario which happens often in services for refugees is of having clients speaking languages where a translation of the service's usual measures does not exist. In this situation it may be perfectly acceptable, even good practice, to use a pilot translation or an approved translation that does not yet have a psychometric exploration, but get the authors' permission to do this if you can. Such pilot translations may help to produce a final approved translation but, until such a translation exists and referential data start to become available based on its use, scores for the clients using the pilot translation can sensibly be used to look at change over time, and, though cautiously, to compare between different clients using the same pilot translation. However, any comparisons with referential data from the measure in another language would be unwise.

People who are blind or who have lost their sight will need questionnaires in Braille or in audio recordings, but we know of few measures available in these formats and could find very little about the psychometrics of such measures, which may well be different from those of the sighted communities.

Adults with acquired deafness generally have no specific obstacles in relation to self-report questionnaires but this should not be assumed to be the case for the Deaf community (i.e. the sign language using community). Sign languages raise particular issues as their vocabularies and grammar are not a linear sequence of symbols on the page but use three-dimensional space and time, so a sign moving away from the signer may mean something quite different from the same moving the other way. This needs particular care to translate well. Although Deaf clients may be able to read a written questionnaire, this may be far from natural or ideal as a way for them to convey their psychological state. Measures are slowly being translated into sign languages and can be successfully delivered with video but as yet there is little empirical exploration of them.

Measures by focus

After the differences by client group, the next most obvious categorisation of measures is by focus (Table 4.3). This overlaps somewhat with the issue of modality as foci are often about clients' problems and this has traditionally been dominated by a focus on psychiatric diagnoses, although clearly problem domains do not have to be equated with diagnoses.

Quality of life measures

There is a long history of development of measures aiming to cover the quality of life (QoL). Within psychological therapies these have similarities with generic/pantheoretical measures and share with them the challenging tension between length and coverage. The number of possible reflections of quality of life is arguably infinite and may be quite personal, hence a measure that attempts to cover it will always be a compromise. Of course, this is true for any measure aspiring to cover outcomes of most therapies, let alone one trying to cover outcomes of *all*

Table 4.3 Measures by their foci

Area	Measure	Comments/notes
Depression	PHQ-9	Used in IAPT
	BDI-I and BDI-II	CBT based
	HADS	For use in context of physical problems
Anxiety	GAD-7	Used in IAPT
	IAPT phobia scales	Used in IAPT
	BAI	CBT based
	HADS	For use in context of physical problems
Interpersonal functioning	IIP	No longer free
	PROQ-II	Free
	WSAS	Used in IAPT
Obsessional compulsive problems	Obsessive Compulsive Inventory	Used in IAPT
Eating disorders and body image concerns	EAT	
	BITE	
	BSQ	Free – see text
Personality/PD	PDQ	

therapies. Two approaches to the measurement of QoL for the therapies are the CORE-6D: a scoring of the CORE-OM, which gives a score in terms of 'quality adjusted life years (QALYs, see below), a concept much used in health economics; and the ReQoL (Recovering Quality of Life) which is a pair of self-report questionnaires of 20 or 10 items developed specifically as a QALY scoring OM.

Proxy measures

The issue of QoL and QALYs brings us to another useful concept when choosing OMs: the idea of a 'proxy measure'. The term originated in cancer outcome research where one obvious outcome sought appeared simple: longer life expectancy. However, although simple to measure, accumulating much data about life after treatment is necessarily slow and expensive so researchers and clinicians, for some cancers, use 'proxy measures': predictors of life expectancy. These might be indicators of tumour load, such as PSA (Prostate Specific Antigen). The key thing about a proxy measure is that it is important only if it does predict what cancer sufferers really want: cure or longer life with some quality of life.

In fact, it seems useful to regard all current therapy OMs as proxy measures: clients do not come to therapy to get their scores on outcome measures down, they come to suffer less, to function better. These are things that the OM may measure quite well, but clients want any change to be robust and to last, and that is not something any instrument can predict. This is not to denigrate immediate change. To help some people move forward is important and we always hope it will be a step to a better life. However, it is not the whole outcome of a therapy, which can only really be judged later.

This brings us back to QALYs. Put simply, health economists believe that we all want as many good quality years to come as possible. The QALY scores from the CORE-6D scoring of a CORE-OM, or from the ReQoL, are a weighting of the current quality of someone's life, and are obviously not a magical prediction of the quality and quantity of the years still to come. However, they turn current state into a multiplier: a proportion compared to a generalised 'full quality life'.

To paraphrase what we said in Chapter 1, few people on their deathbeds will wish they had spent more time self-rating, and no one will have a single 'number' that they believe to be the 'outcome' of their lives. Nevertheless, having good proxy measures *and not overrating them* can help us to improve therapies.

Case examples of measures

Having covered some of the categories of measures and issues, we will use a few case examples that we hope will help you when choosing OMs or appraising ones you must use in your service. We will look at a general measure, a specific measure, a very short measure and a mixed-methods measure.

A general measure: CORE-OM, its short forms and scoring

We have chosen to use the CORE-OM as an example as it is the measure with which we are most familiar, having been involved in its development from the beginning in 1995. The acronym CORE - Clinical Outcomes in Routine Evaluation - is also obviously close to the philosophy of this book and the 'OM' stands for 'Outcome Measure'. The CORE-OM is a 34-item self-report questionnaire specifically designed to be used to measure change in any form of psychological therapy - i.e. it is pantheoretical. It was designed after reviewing other measures and reports of experience of using existing measures which, with the exception of the GHQ (General Health Questionnaire), were problem-specific or diagnosis-focused measures. The aims in the grant specification that shaped the CORE-OM were that the measure should be free to reproduce without a licence fee ('copyleft'), that it should cover the domains of risk, well-being, problems and functioning, and that it should have both intrapsychic and interpersonal items. Finally, the specification required that it be short enough for use in routine practice. The CORE-OM in English is reproduced in full on the next two pages.

If you do not know the CORE-OM, do read through it and score yourself, and then imagine clients you know completing it. Then think about some clients you have worked with whom you feel changed positively in therapy and imagine how their completion of the measure might have changed from the first to the last session. Then try doing the same for someone who did not seem to do well with therapy (no therapist or therapy helps everyone). We imagine that you will notice that items will differ in pertinence to different clients. As noted above, there is a scoring using six items from the CORE-OM – the CORE-6D – which converts responses into a quality of life rating (QoL) based on data from a UK population. There are translations of the CORE-OM into 25 languages, including British Sign Language. Remember, however, that it should not be assumed that referential score distributions or the CORE-6D scoring will be the same for the CORE-OM used in other languages or cultures.

A specific measure: Body Shape Questionnaire (BSQ)

The BSQ shares having 34 items with the CORE-OM but is otherwise radically different as all its items focus on one issue: concerns about body shape. The concerns are those that became seemingly endemic, particularly in younger women in many Western countries through the 20th century, and which are seen in extreme forms in anorexia nervosa and bulimia nervosa. The items are conceptually 'unidimensional', i.e. will show high internal reliability (Chapter 3): people who score high on one item are extremely likely to score high on all other items. This will not be the same, not to the same extent, for short, broad coverage measures like the CORE-OM or OQ-45 where it is likely that subgroups of people will have more problems in some domains within the coverage of the measure and others may have more problems in other domains.

Even single diagnosis measures like the PHQ-9 and GAD-7 may not show unidimensionality because there is more heterogeneity of depressive issues and of anxiety issues than there is in body shape concerns. Strongly unidimensional measures are particularly suited to the development of multiple short forms, which will show very strong consistency of psychometrics across forms and allow users to pick a length that suits them. For example, long ones when the body shape concerns are the only focus and high reliability and score range are wanted, and shorter ones where body shape concerns are only one of a number of things you want to measure. There are two 16-item and four 8-item short forms of the BSQ. Short forms of OMs are sometimes used to address the familiarity that clients develop with items as the different versions can be changed across repeated completions to minimise recognition of items and the issues that might arise if people try to remember what they ticked the last time. The Body Shape Questionnaire (BSQ) and its short forms are available at PSYCTC.org (2021).

CORE-OM

Site ID: | Age
Client ID: | Gender: M F
Therapist ID:
Date form given: D D M M Y Y Y Y

Stage Completed:
S Screening
R Referral
A Assessment
F First Therapy Session
P Pre-therapy (unspecified)
D During Therapy
L Last therapy session
X Follow up 1
Y Follow up 2

Stage | Episode

IMPORTANT - PLEASE READ THIS FIRST

This form has 34 statements about how you have been **OVER THE LAST WEEK**.
Please read each statement and think how often you felt that way last week.
Then tick the box which is closest to this.

Over the last week ...

		Not at all	Only occasionally	Sometimes	Often	Most or all the time	OFFICE USE ONLY
1	I have felt terribly alone and isolated	0	1	2	3	4	F
2	I have felt tense, anxious or nervous	0	1	2	3	4	P
3	I have felt I have someone to turn to for support when needed	4	3	2	1	0	F
4	I have felt O.K. about myself	4	3	2	1	0	W
5	I have felt totally lacking in energy and enthusiasm	0	1	2	3	4	P
6	I have been physically violent to others	0	1	2	3	4	R
7	I have felt able to cope when things go wrong	4	3	2	1	0	F
8	I have been troubled by aches, pains or other physical problems	0	1	2	3	4	P
9	I have thought of hurting myself	0	1	2	3	4	R
10	Talking to people has felt too much for me	0	1	2	3	4	F
11	Tension and anxiety have prevented me doing important things	0	1	2	3	4	P
12	I have been happy with the things I have done	4	3	2	1	0	F
13	I have been disturbed by unwanted thoughts and feelings	0	1	2	3	4	P
14	I have felt like crying	0	1	2	3	4	W

Please turn over

eng Page1

Figure 4.1 Page 1 of the CORE-OM (CORE-OM, 2020)

Over the last week ...

		Not at all	Only occasionally	Sometimes	Often	Most or all the time	OFFICE USE ONLY
15	I have felt panic or terror	0	1	2	3	4	P
16	I made plans to end my life	0	1	2	3	4	R
17	I have felt overwhelmed by my problems	0	1	2	3	4	W
18	I have had difficulty getting to sleep or staying asleep	0	1	2	3	4	P
19	I have felt warmth or affection for someone	4	3	2	1	0	F
20	My problems have been impossible to put to one side	0	1	2	3	4	P
21	I have been able to do most things I needed to	4	3	2	1	0	F
22	I have threatened or intimidated another person	0	1	2	3	4	R
23	I have felt despairing or hopeless	0	1	2	3	4	P
24	I have thought it would be better if I were dead	0	1	2	3	4	R
25	I have felt criticised by other people	0	1	2	3	4	F
26	I have thought I have no friends	0	1	2	3	4	F
27	I have felt unhappy	0	1	2	3	4	P
28	Unwanted images or memories have been distressing me	0	1	2	3	4	P
29	I have been irritable when with other people	0	1	2	3	4	F
30	I have thought I am to blame for my problems and difficulties	0	1	2	3	4	P
31	I have felt optimistic about my future	4	3	2	1	0	W
32	I have achieved the things I wanted to	4	3	2	1	0	F
33	I have felt humiliated or shamed by other people	0	1	2	3	4	F
34	I have hurt myself physically or taken dangerous risks with my health	0	1	2	3	4	R

THANK YOU FOR YOUR TIME IN COMPLETING THIS QUESTIONNAIRE

	(W)	(P)	(F)	(R)	All items	All minus R
Total Scores						
Mean Scores (Total score for each dimension divided by number of items completed in that dimension)						

eng

Page 2

Figure 4.2 Page 2 of the CORE-OM (CORE-OM, 2020)

Very short measures: Patient Health Questionnaire (PHQ-9) and General Anxiety Disorder 7 (GAD-7)

The PHQ-9 is, as the name suggests, a 9-item questionnaire that essentially takes the diagnostic criteria for a diagnosis of depression from DSM-IV and converts them into self-report form. The General Anxiety Disorder 7 (GAD-7) is a closely related measure using the DSM-IV criteria for General Anxiety Disorder. In line with the DSM criteria, both the PHQ-9 and GAD-7 ask about the frequency of issues over the preceding two weeks. The PHQ-9 is available at: www.phqscreeners.com/ and both are copyright to the pharmaceutical company Pfizer, who currently make them available for free (although without any legal undertaking to continue to do so forever).

Again, if you do not know these measures, you might want to read through them and do the same exercise of imagining initial and final completions for yourself or some of your clients that we suggested for the CORE-OM.

A mixed-methods measure: PSYCHLOPS

PSYCHLOPS is radically different from the questionnaires described above, being (largely) a 'client-generated measure' and one that specifically rates the issues the client themselves identify as being troublesome. It was based on the MYMOP (Measure Yourself Medical Outcome Profile), which was designed for physical health issues. Both PSYCHLOPS and MYMOP ask the client to name or describe something that has been troubling them over the last week and they then offer the option to add another problem and then ask for a way in which the problem or problems are impacting on the person's life. Each of those items is rated for 'how much it has affected you' on a 0 to 5 scale. Finally, there is a single nomothetic item 'How have you felt in yourself over the last week?', also rated 0 to 5. The score is the mean of the completed items (i.e. scaled from 0 to 5 regardless of whether one or two problems are volunteered). The last, a nomothetic item, makes PSYCHLOPS a hybrid rather than a pure client-generated measure. The measure can be repeated during or at the end of therapy when the initial problems and impacts are presented back to the respondent to re-rate. The version for use during therapy allows for the addition of a new problem as the therapy progresses and the nature of the problems concerning the client change. The measures are available at: http://psychlops.org.uk/

Again, if you do not know this measure, do go through the same exercise of imagining it being used. What new problems might clients have added to their initial problems if using the within-therapy form? How do you feel the clients' problems might have mapped to any CORE-OM, PHQ-9 or GAD-7 items, or to anything on the BSQ?

What do these examples tell us about measures?

This is certainly not a comprehensive overview of measures. There are large books of questionnaires and, as mentioned earlier in this chapter, the Department of Health compendium, although archived by the DoH, remains a good, extensive guide. Our aim is to invite you to look at a few selected measures and think about how they compare, what features are shared and what differences there are, and how measures fit into the different categories of OMs that are available.

We believe that completing the measures yourself is vital to understand what your clients' experiences might be and to counter the general tendencies to equate our OMs with thermometers or weighing scales. We believe that anyone who imagines a number of clients using these measures can see the psychological complexity of answering them, which helps us to stop treating them as if they were physical science measurements.

Thinking through the completion of measures will reveal potential issues that can and will arise with any measure. Try not to simply reject them, but to use this to think more deeply about the experience of using the measure and to consider the many things that therapists and clients can gain when therapists drop either idealisation or denigration of OMs. We find that thinking of different clients underlines that no measure is perfect for all the issues that any client brings to therapy. However, we also find that it can be interesting to discover that most clients that we feel did make improvement during therapy *would* have shown improvement on general and on client-generated measures. Indeed, many would have shown improvement on the PHQ-9 or GAD-7 (but only if their problems had included those diagnostic foci of depression or anxiety). However, only those with body shape and eating concerns would have improved much on the BSQ. This reminds us of the obvious difference between general and specific measures.

Therapeutic alliance and process measures

There are many measures you might have heard of that have not been mentioned in this chapter. Many will not be therapy OMs but have a focus, for example, in the therapeutic relationship or the process of therapy. A number of measures address the therapeutic alliance and there is evidence that a good therapeutic alliance is correlated with outcomes, and some evidence that resolving alliance ruptures in therapy also predicts outcomes. However, we are not exploring these measures here as we want to have a clear separation of OMs from the wide field of process measures.

Practicalities

When selecting the measures that are right for your clients and your practice or service, it will help to use the general frameworks introduced in Chapters

2 and 3, and especially 'GULP': those are generic issues that apply to any measure. However, sitting on top of those, logistics and practicalities are always crucial. The following list may look obvious but overlooking these issues can really impair data collection.

- Are you using paper or electronic copies of the measures?
- What do you need to do to get them ready?
- If you are using electronic copies of the measures, where is the interface? Will it always be there? How can you make that convenient?
- If you are using paper copies of the measures, where will you store the measures and when and how do you replenish your supplies? What triggers a new order or making more copies? (Yes, it really matters: no measures = no scores!)
- Do you give them to the client before the session, in the session itself or after it?
- If using paper, are completed forms given to you or to a secretary/receptionist, or placed in a box?
- If you are using the measures for outcome measurement rather than embedded change measurement you should probably choose not to see the scores. So how do you make sure that the client knows this? How will the client be identified on the measure? This must be clear as you are not seeing the OM being completed. What process do you have for ensuring that the ID coding will map client to data collection in a reliable way and that you ensure anonymity for the individual?
- How will they be analysed? That means computerisation, so if the OM is on paper, who enters the data into what program?
- When the data is entered, by transcribing or directly by the client, is the data backed up and safe against loss? Is it completely confidential and secure from inappropriate access?

As we said in earlier chapters, good and ethical use of outcome and change measures in practice is always rooted in the clients' understanding of why you are doing what you are doing, and their understanding of what will happen to their data. This does not require the elaborate information and consent forms that would be expected in a formal research study, but it will make a huge difference to clients' use of the measures if an honest and confident explanation of these things is given and it is an ethical and legal obligation to do this.

Summary

In this chapter we have introduced to you to the different categories of outcome and change measures that you may come across with your clients or in services you are linked to. We do not think it would be appropriate for us to recommend specific measures as this book is geared to giving you the tools to make those choices for yourself. This will be different for practitioners with different caseloads, who see different groups of clients, who work alone or with others, and who have different questions that they want to ask of the data that they collect. Hopefully, by the end of the book you will feel more confident to identify the categories of measures you may be interested in using, and then to examine and judge the practical utility of them for your purpose as well as being able to examine and judge their psychometric qualities.

5

Analysing change data from outcome measures

Introduction

This chapter takes us to numbers. We use examples of datasets to illustrate the kinds of statistics and procedures that you will come across when reading research and audit reports. We describe the main tools used and explain why data are presented the way they are and show you how to interpret graphs and datasets. We know some people find numbers and statistics scary, but we hope to give you some confidence with them.

At its heart, measuring change is easy: simply subtract the starting score from the finishing score and there is your change. Take someone who started with a score of 23 and finished on 6: you have a clear change score of 17. Any of us can do that sort of arithmetic. However, things get more complicated if you have many clients' scores and if you want to know, statistically, whether these changes mean anything collectively. Although most therapists can remember with remarkable clarity and detail the stories of their clients, most of us do not remember numbers with the same ease - particularly when we are thinking about the scores of, say, 50 clients. For this we need some tools: procedures for handling numbers and statistical methods. In this chapter we will give you a grasp of such procedures and an introduction to statistics.

Moving from numbers to statistics: starting with procedures

Theory can help us both make sense of and remember the data of our clients' stories. How does an early deprivation get repeated in subsequent relationships? Is there an ABC (antecedents - behaviour - consequences) pattern to the main problems? Just as clinical theory can help us to hold onto clients' narratives, these statistical methods help us to hold pictures of data and enable us to draw out the meaning from them. There are no perfect representational systems: just as psychotherapy theory, used clumsily, can get in the way of listening properly to any individual client's story, so can quantitative methods, if used incautiously, obscure what matters in numerical data. As with clinical theory, the challenge is to get the balance right and this chapter is all about trying to help you do that.

Procedures 1: tabulation

Statistics is about handling lots of data and about coping with uncertainty and noise in your data. That starts with some fairly simple procedures to describe and summarise sets of numbers. Going back to our single client example above, we had those two scores (23 and 6) with the one change score (-17). What if we consider more clients? One fundamental procedure to handle multiple numbers is tabulation. Table 5.1 shows us what that might look like for 10 clients from a fictional stepped-care service. It sets out variables we might want to consider when looking at change: gender, number of sessions initially offered, any 'did not attends' (DNAs), cancellations, how many sessions were actually attended, pre and post scores on a change measure, and the raw difference (change) in those scores.

Table 5.1 Table of data (n = 10)

ID	Gender	Offered	DNA	Canc	Attend	pre	post	change
1	M	24	1	2	21	15	8	–7
2	F	6	1	0	5	23	15	–8
3	F	24	1	1	22	23	18	–5
4	F	6	0	0	6	17	14	–3
5	F	6	1	0	5	25	24	–1
6	M	24	3	0	21	35	13	–22
7	F	6	1	0	5	34	26	–8
8	F	24	0	2	22	31	20	–11
9	F	6	1	1	4	21	21	0
10	F	6	0	0	6	22	23	1

Procedures 2: summary numbers, descriptive statistics

Even with only 10 clients and nine variables that is a lot to summarise and explore. Descriptive statistics summarise data. Two of the simplest statistics are the maximum and the minimum. Without too much difficulty, we can see in Table 5.1 that 35 was the highest starting score in that dataset (the maximum), 15 was the lowest starting score (minimum); the procedure that gives us the maximum and minimum is just sorting. The maximum and minimum final scores were 26 and 8 respectively. Table 5.2 takes the same data but sorted by the final scores.

Table 5.2 Sorted scores

ID	Offered	DNA	Canc	Attend	pre	post	change
7	6	1	0	5	34	26	–8
5	6	1	0	5	25	24	–1
10	6	0	0	6	22	23	1
9	6	1	1	4	21	21	0
8	24	0	2	22	31	20	–11
3	24	1	1	22	23	18	–5
2	6	1	0	5	23	15	–8
4	6	0	0	6	17	14	–3
6	24	3	0	21	35	13	–22
1	24	1	2	21	15	8	–7
Mean:	13.2	0.9	0.6	11.7	24.6	18.2	–6.4
SD:	9.3	0.9	0.8	8.5	6.8	5.7	6.7

So, maximum and minimum are very simple statistics referring to aspects of a set of data. Table 5.2 adds some more summaries to the data at the bottom. The most famous statistic is probably the mean ('arithmetic mean' to statisticians, 'average' to most of us). The mean initial score here is 24.6 and the mean final score is 18.2. We are used to the idea that the mean is one number that summarises a collection of numbers. The mean describes the centre of gravity, or 'central location', of that set of numbers. We have put the means for each variable at the bottom of their columns in the table.

Beneath those means we have also added the standard deviation (SD) for the scores. While the mean is an indicator of central location, the SD is a measure of the scatter of the numbers around that central location. If all 10 starting scores had been 7.1, the SD would have been zero. It is not that difficult to understand the maths of the mean, but the SD is a bit more complicated and we only need to know it measures scatter around the mean. Of course, it makes no sense to summarise gender with a mean: categories are summarised by counts, proportions or percentages. Looking at Table 5.1, we see that the proportion of the clients who were male is 0.2 (20%).

Therapy data can be values on a scale, categories or counts. We now have a table that has both raw scale data and summaries: the means and SDs of that raw data. Sometimes tables, especially ones of large datasets, only contain summaries and no raw data. Table 5.1 also has categorical data - gender - and count data - numbers of sessions. There is nothing esoteric about this: you buy some things by weight (continuous variable) - 'can I have 500g of that cheese?' - and other things by number - 'can I have five of those muffins?' - or by category - apples or pears. Table 5.3 summarises variable types.

Table 5.3 Variable types

Variable type	Description	Everyday examples	Routine Outcome Measurement (ROM) or therapy examples	Non-ROM therapy examples
Scaled or continuous	How much!	Weight of flour; volume of water; length of yarn	OM score (start OR end); age; weight; time	Total duration of speech turn by client and by therapist
Categorical	Which (type)!	Type of cheese or fruit; profession; town	Modality; gender; format (e.g. individual, couple/ family or group)	'Step 2' or 'Step 3', e.g. short- or long-term therapies in stepped care
Counts	How many!	1,2,3,4,5......	No. of OMs completed; DNAs	Number of sessions attended

Sometimes data makes more sense because of the relationship one variable has to another: Table 5.4 takes the attendance variables from Table 5.1 and makes them more informative by looking at the attendance, DNA and cancellation counts against the counts of sessions offered.

Now it can be seen that the overall percentage of sessions offered that were attended was 87.6%. You can also see that some summaries make more sense than others: it is true that the mean number of sessions offered was 13.2 but that is not a very informative summary when we see that there were two very different numbers of sessions offered in the service, either 24 or 6. (It is the big difference between those two that makes for the high SD - showing the high scatter around their mean.)

Tables become easier to read with practice and a good table should be clearly labelled and explained in the accompanying text so that it is understandable. Good tables should be no harder to read and understand than a bank statement, although you may find that some of the more complex tables

Table 5.4 Attendance percentages

ID	Offered	DNA	%DNA	Canc	%Canc	Attend	%Attend
1	24	1	4%	2	8%	21	88%
2	6	1	17%	0	0%	5	83%
3	24	1	4%	1	4%	22	92%
4	6	0	0%	0	0%	6	100%
5	6	1	17%	0	0%	5	83%
6	24	3	12%	0	0%	21	88%
7	6	1	17%	0	0%	5	83%
8	24	0	0%	2	8%	22	92%
9	6	1	17%	1	17%	4	67%
10	6	0	0%	0	0%	6	100%
Mean:	13.2	0.9	8.8%	0.6	3.7%	11.7	87.6%
SD:	9.3	0.9	7.9%	0.8	5.7%	8.5	9.6%

in academic research reports seem somewhat inscrutable and may need quite a bit of care and re-checking to be understood.

So, tables can be very helpful in setting out a summary of the data and may contain only raw data, raw data with summaries, or just summaries.

Procedures 3: visualising with graphs and plots

The other main procedures to summarise quantitative data are plots or graphs. As with tables, familiarity will make it easier to interpret graphs. Graphs, even more than tables, can take many forms. In this book we will introduce you to five plots that we think are among the most useful for OM data. These are: cat's cradle plots, scattergrams (including Jacobson plots), histograms, boxplots and forest plots.

Cat's cradle plot

Figure 5.1 is an example of a line plot, specifically what we call a 'cat's cradle plot' (after the children's game). This plots the starting and final score data from Table 5.1.

As with most graphs you will meet, this graph uses two axes to present data. Here the vertical (y) axis shows us the scores on the measure, whereas the horizontal (x) axis shows us points in time (first and last session).

Looking at the graph, we can see how it turns the scores from Table 5.1 into visual form showing the trajectory of change for each client with each client

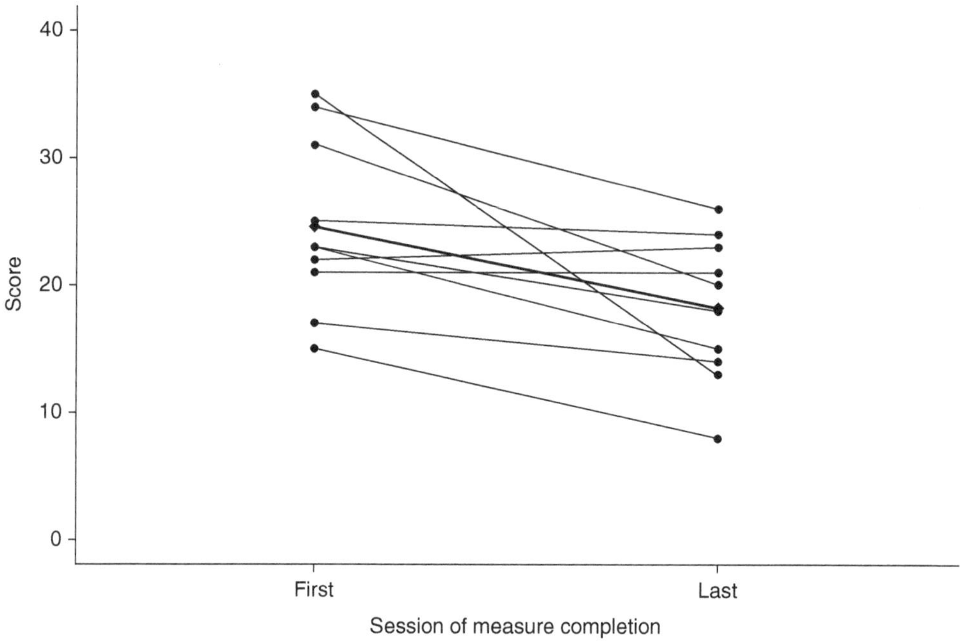

Figure 5.1 Simple cat's cradle plot

shown by a line with circles at each end. We can see the steepest drop is for the client whose scores dropped from 35 to 13; we can also see that only one client showed a deterioration in scores (from 22 to 23) and that one client showed no change at all, starting and finishing on 21. The graph adds a summary of the data showing the mean initial and final scores as diamonds joined by thicker line than for the individual clients. In these data there was a mean improvement in scores from 24.6 to 18.2, as in Table 5.2.

Another plot that is widely used to summarise therapy change data is the 'Jacobson plot'. This plot will introduce the terms 'reliable change' and 'clinically significant change', which are widely used in ROM, so we will go through these and build the plot.

The reliable change index is a methodology for assessing whether the change between scores for any one client is robust, specifically that it is unlikely to have arisen by chance fluctuations arising from the unreliability of the measure. 'Clinically significant change' is a term used to describe change taking a client's score from one typical of a dysfunctional or clinical group to one typical of a functional, non-clinical group. These are very useful ways of commenting on whether changes observed in clients' scores mean something. The next four graphs build up the Jacobson plot using the same data from Table 5.1 and the cat's cradle plot in Figure 5.1.

Figure 5.2 shows end of therapy (y axis) finishing scores plotted against the starting scores (x axis). The client with most change (35 to 13) is plotted with

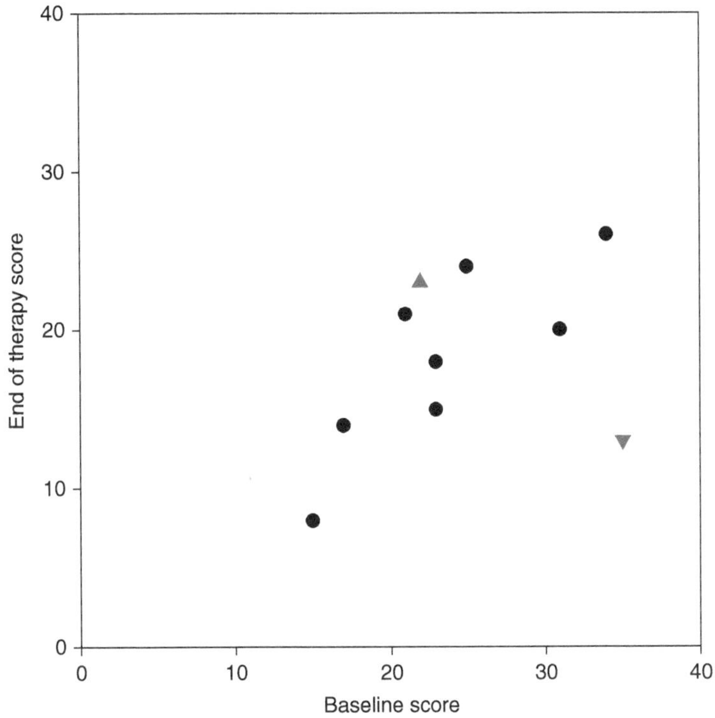

Figure 5.2 Pre-Jacobson plot: scattergram of final against starting scores

the grey, downward pointing triangle and the client with the greatest deterioration in scores (22 to 23) with the grey upward pointing triangle.

Figure 5.3 shows the next development, in looking at the same data: we have simply added the 'leading diagonal' line to the plot. Any person on this line has shown no score change at all, as for our person whose initial and final scores were both 21. People who showed improvement, i.e. a drop in scores, show as points below that line and clients who showed deterioration are above the line. Again, this shows us something about the differences in the data. Adding the line simplifies identifying the person with no score change and the one client who showed deterioration. Below the line, the further away from the line the clients' points lie, the more improvement in their scores, hence the one person who moved from 35 to 13 lies furthest from the line.

The next stage (Figure 5.4) is to add the idea of 'reliable change' that Jacobson and his colleagues introduced. Reliable change is about whether people have changed enough that the change is unlikely to be due to unreliability of measurement. As discussed in Chapter 3, a good measure should produce similar scores when measuring the same thing. However, as OMs are real measures, not magical ones, they always have measurement unreliability and even measuring 'the same state' (if we could define that) would not give exactly the same score every time. Reliable change is defined as change that would

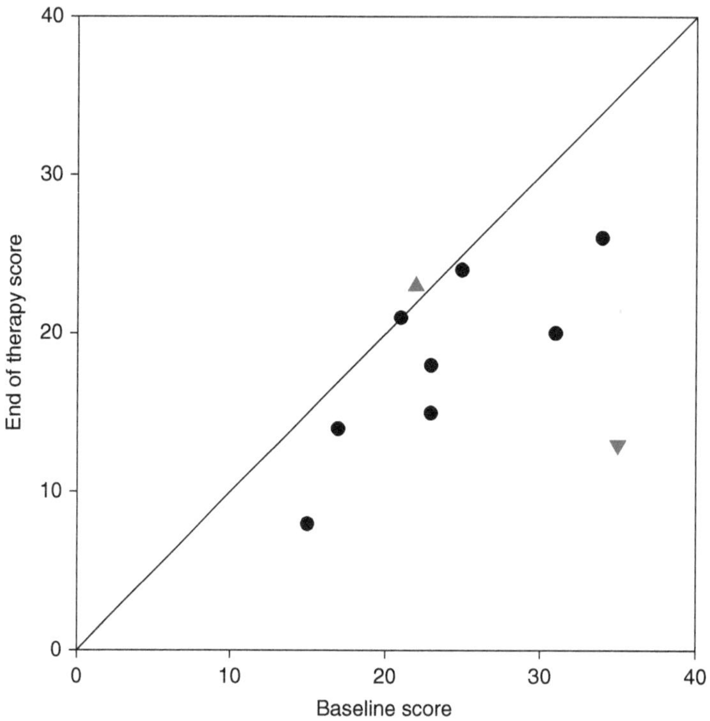

Figure 5.3 Pre-Jacobson plot: scattergram with leading diagonal

occur less than 5% of the time if the only change that happened came from measurement unreliability; if that were so 2.5% would show deterioration, i.e. above, and 2.5% improvement, i.e. below the leading diagonal line that marks no change. Figure 5.4 now shows us that three clients showed score changes inside that area of unreliability, including the one whose initial and final scores were exactly the same and the one whose scores deteriorated.

However, for seven of the clients the score change seems to be greater than you would expect from measurement unreliability alone and all seven in our simulated data show reliable improvement.

OK, one more step to go. As well as introducing the concept of 'reliable change', Jacobson and his colleagues also introduced the idea of 'clinically significant change' (CSC). This is thought of as change that takes someone from a score typical of a *clinical population* to a score typical of a *non-clinical population*. For real OMs there are good ways of determining sensible values for Jacobson's CSC. For these fictional data we put it at 17.5 and add that to our plot and we have the final Jacobson plot (Figure 5.5).

Now that the CSC for the starting score is the vertical reference line from 17.5 on the x axis and that for the final score is the horizontal reference line, we can see that the seven clients who showed reliable improvements in scores fall into three groups. In the pale grey area, there are two clients who have

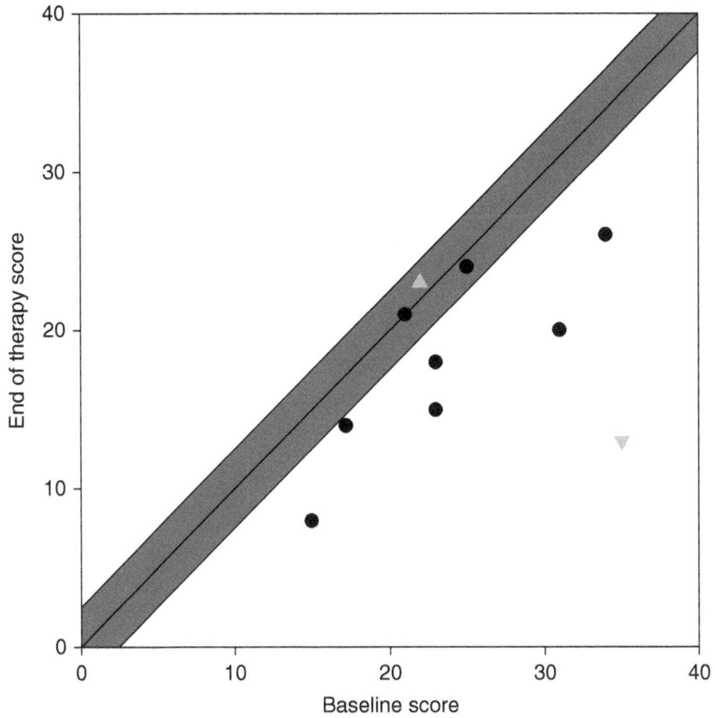

Figure 5.4 Pre-Jacobson plot: scattergram with diagonal and RCI tramlines

shown reliable change *and* dropped from a score above the clinical threshold (CSC) to one below it. The client whose scores dropped most, marked with the triangle, is one of these. On the bottom left of the graph, there are two clients whose initial scores started below the clinical cutting point. This means that they cannot show CSC, although they have shown reliable improvement (otherwise their scores would be in the grey tramlines). Finally, we have a third group in the upper right area of the graph: these three clients have shown reliable improvement in their scores, but their final scores remain in the clinical range.

There are essentially an infinite number ways of plotting data. The cat's cradle plot and the Jacobson plot are both variants of scattergrams. Scattergrams map scores on two variables with the two scores defining the location of the points. The cat's cradle plot shows scores against time, the Jacobson plot shows final scores against baseline scores. We will meet other scattergrams later in this chapter and in Chapter 8. The other plots we find most useful are the histogram, the boxplot and the forest plot, and we will come to these after discussing the move from small (so far, $n = 10$) datasets to larger ones. Each of these plots has particular strengths, but like all data handling procedures they aim to simplify the data in one way in order to make some aspect of it clear.

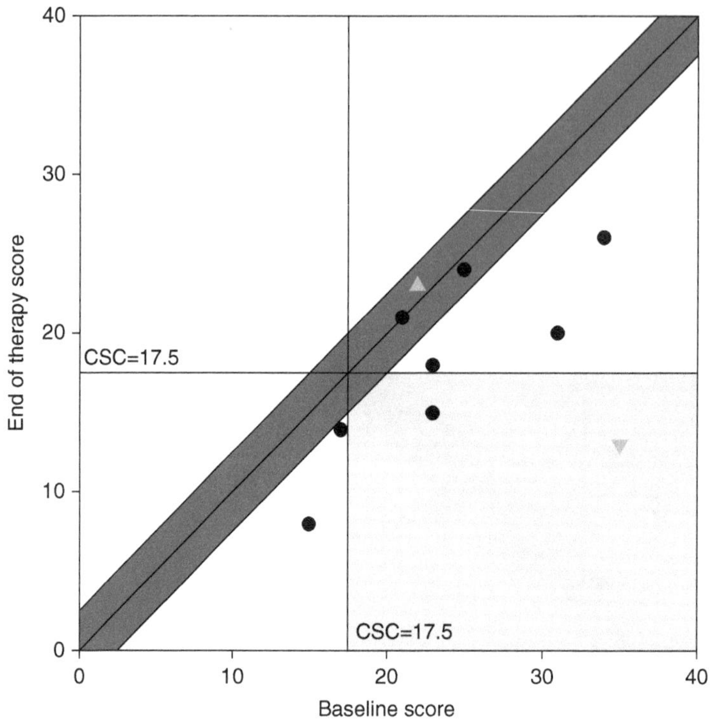

Figure 5.5 Finished Jacobson plot

Looking at larger datasets

We started this chapter with a small dataset to make it easy to count the numbers and map the clients in the tables to their scores in the plots. We hope that made it easy enough to follow the summarising and plotting. However, with many clients in a dataset, counting by hand stops being feasible and we turn to computers to handle the data.

The following plots illustrate this. Figure 5.6 shows fictional data from four years of work of a single therapist, who has seen 240 clients for between 2 and 25 sessions. Each client's initial and final OM scores are shown on the y axis and the number of sessions on the x axis to give a time-stretched cat's cradle plot. 'Time-stretched' as, unlike the cat's cradle plot in Figure 5.1 where the axis ignored numbers of sessions and just showed first and last scores, this shows the time between those scores.

The challenge in reading Figure 5.6 is 'overprinting', which arises when the amount of data means data points overlap or completely obscure each other. Figure 5.6 avoids the loss of information caused by overprinting by using circles whose area reflects the number of clients with exactly the same scores and numbers of sessions. The legend below the plot indicates how size of circle increases for numbers of clients.

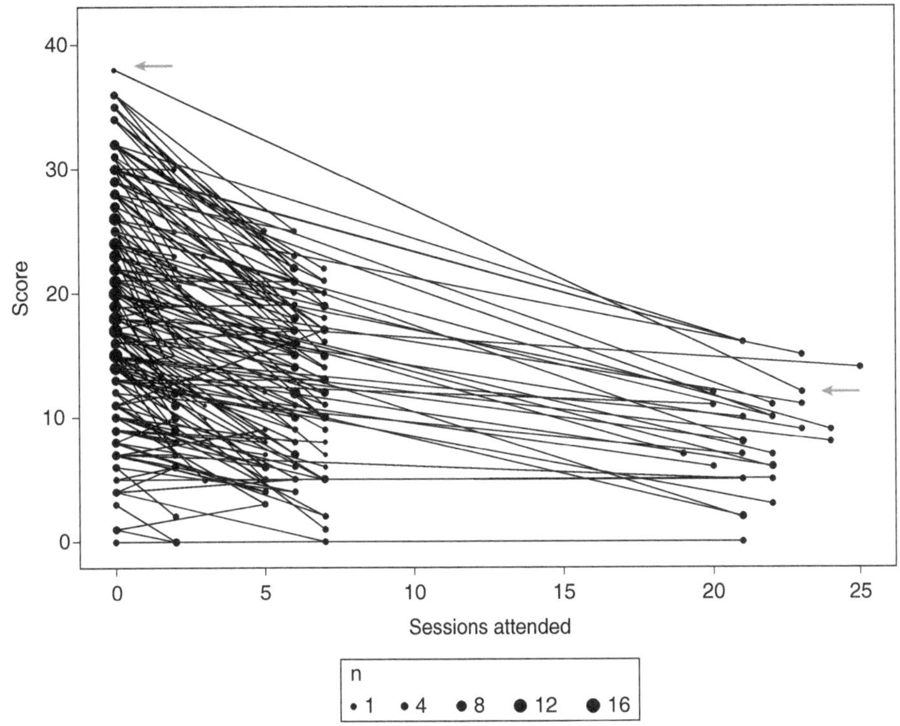

Figure 5.6 Time-stretched cat's cradle plot

Figure 5.7 shows exactly the same data but in a Jacobson plot.

Staying with the cat's cradle plot for a moment, again, where more than one client has the same pair of starting and ending scores as another client, the plot uses the area of the plotting circles to show the numbers of clients with those scores. Two grey arrows in Figure 5.6 show the starting and final scores of the client whose score dropped most, here from a score of 38 to a score of 12. This same person is the point on the far right of the Jacobson plot in Figure 5.7, marked by the grey arrow.

The cat's cradle plot in Figure 5.6 tells us about any relationship between score change and numbers of sessions and the Jacobson plot in Figure 5.7 ignores the number of sessions but gives a clearer sense of breakdown of score changes across all 240 clients. From that plot we can see that the general tendency was for scores to improve, to drop below the leading diagonal. We can also see that there was one client (above the dark grey tramlines) who showed reliable deterioration but that s/he started and finished below the clinical cut-off score starting at a score of 11 and finishing at a score of 17. We can see there were a number of clients who stayed in the 'no reliable change' tramlines of the 5% allowance we make for the measure not having perfect reliability. There are actually 39 of them but it's not easy to count that number from the plot. Thirty-nine is well below 95% of 240 (228), so clearly this plot is not just showing score change caused by unreliability of measurement.

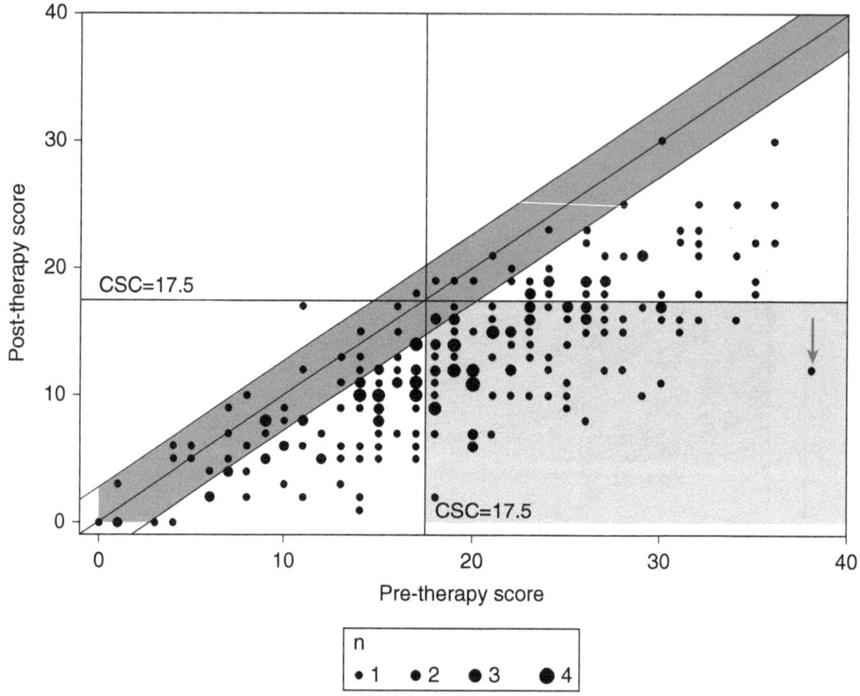

Figure 5.7 Jacobson plot of change (n = 240)

Two hundred showed reliable improvement, i.e. their points lie below the leading diagonal. We certainly cannot count them from the plot but we know there are 240 in all and one showed reliable deterioration, and as we have also said there were 39 no reliable change, we can work out the 200 as 240-1-39. Again, this is dramatically more than the six (2.5% of 240) that we would have expected had all change been merely down to unreliability of measurement.

We can see how plotting the larger dataset in this way gives a good picture to convey the pattern of change – it helps us to see the wood for the trees.

Table 5.5 Table of reliable and clinically significant change (numbers)

	Reliable deterioration	No reliable change	Reliable improvement	Total
Clinically significant deterioration	0	1	–	1
Stayed clinical	0	7	39	46
Stayed non-clinical	1	28	70	99
Clinically significant improvement	–	3	91	94
Total	1	39	200	240

To really get the best out of routine change measurement we need to get into the habit of looking into graphs like this. However, although we did manage to get the precise counts of clients in the categories from the plot, that is clearly not the strength of the plot: to get that detail we go back to tabulating the data but choosing a way that is easy to read (with practice) and tells us things we want to know. Table 5.5 shows that Jacobson plot turned into a table.

In the second column of the table, we can see the one client who showed reliable deterioration but stayed in the non-clinical range; this is the one client who was visible above the tramlines in Figure 5.7.

In column 3, we can see that the 39 clients in the 'no reliable change' tramlines, can be subdivided into:

- one who showed clinically significant deterioration (i.e. moved from below to above the clinical cut-off scores: the single point in the little triangular part within the tramlines, just above and to the left of the intersection of the pre and post cutting lines in the Jacobson plot in Figure 5.7);
- seven who stayed in the clinical range (between the tramlines but above and to the right of the intersection of the cutting points in Figure 5.7);
- twenty-eight who stayed in the non-clinical range (between the tramlines but below and to the left of the intersection of the cutting points in Figure 5.7); and, finally,
- three who moved from clinical to non-clinical (the single point and circle for two people in the grey triangle below and to the right of the intersection of the cutting points).

Similarly, in the fourth column of the table, we can see that 200 clients showed *reliable* improvement, but of these, 39 stayed in the clinical score range so did not show clinically significant change and 70 stayed in the non-clinical range, leaving 91 who showed both clinically significant and reliable change (in the lighter shaded shaded area on Figure 5.7).

Two cells in that table are marked '–' as they are impossible combinations: it is not possible to have deteriorated *and* improved, nor vice versa!

Table 5.6 gives exactly the same data but using percentages.

Table 5.6 Table of reliable and clinically significant change (percentages)

	Reliable deterioration	No reliable change	Reliable improvement	Total
Clinically significant deterioration	0.0%	0.4%	–	0.4%
Stayed clinical	0.0%	2.9%	16.2%	19.1%
Stayed non-clinical	0.4%	11.7%	29.2%	41.3%
Clinically significant improvement	–	1.2%	37.9%	39.1%
Total	0.4%	16.2%	83.3%	99.9%

Reflecting on the data we have been discussing, it is important to remember that these data are from a simulation to illustrate the different elements of reliable change and clinically significant change that we wanted to explain. They may not, therefore, be typical of clinical services. For example, in many services some or all of those who scored in the non-clinical score range might not have been taken on for therapy.

Aggregating and summarising data with ratios: odds and odds ratios

For count data, as we have just seen in Table 5.5, we often summarise counts in terms of proportions, and in Table 5.6 these were shown as percentages. These are so familiar to all of us that we did not need to explain them. However, in research papers you may see count data talked of in terms of 'odds'. If you like gambling you may be very familiar with this. If the odds on a horse winning are said to be '50 to 1 against', then the prediction is that the horse has a 1 in 51 chance of winning, and if the odds are said to be '2 to 1 on', then the prediction is that the horse has a 2 in 3 chance of winning. Talking in terms of odds rather than in terms of proportions or probabilities leads to easier maths for bookies, gamblers and statisticians. We will come back to this in Chapter 7, but Table 5.7 is a very simple table to see if there is a gender difference in our larger dataset in allocation to steps 2 or 3.

Table 5.7 Gender odds ratio by stepped care step

Gender	Step 2	Step 3	Proportion	%	Odds ratio
F	130	26	0.83	83.3%	5.0
M	70	14	0.83	83.3%	5.0

The rows break the 240 clients down by gender and then show that exactly the same proportion, .83, i.e. 83% of women and men are allocated to step 2 and to 3. The odds ratio of women to men is 5 for each step level.

Aggregating and summarising the data: more summary statistics

As we have seen, summary statistics are numbers that summarise information in the data and provide shorthand descriptions of it. We have also seen that statistics describing the central location and the scatter of scaled variables like age or OM scores are almost always a sensible starting point in describing and analysing large datasets. Sometimes you will come across the median as the statistic for central location rather than the mean. The median is the value that divides the scores into two equal-sized groups and is another measure of central location.

It describes the mid-point in a set of numbers ordered consecutively and it is useful where there are extreme or outlier scores. For example, it may be more useful to know that 50% of clients attend for three sessions than to know that the mean number of sessions attended is 19, which might be the case in a service where most people attend for a few sessions, but a subgroup attend for more than a year. As always with data, the choice is about finding the most useful summary for the distribution of data. That brings us to one of the best graphs to describe the distribution of data: the histogram.

Histograms

A histogram gives a very complete description of the distribution of one variable. Figure 5.8 is a histogram of the number of sessions attended by all clients attending a large service.

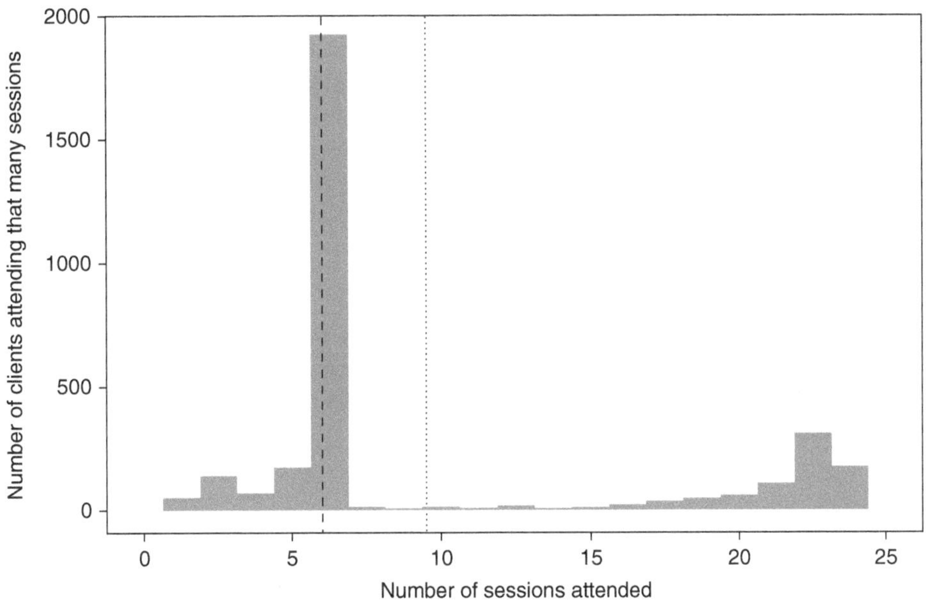

Figure 5.8 Histogram of attendance

The histogram gives us a visual illustration that contains all the information about the number of attendances in the service. In Figure 5.8 we can see that the x axis is the number of sessions attended and the y axis shows the numbers of clients attending that many sessions. We can see that the session count does not include zero, so presumably the service is not counting clients who were offered an appointment but never attended. Although the x axis goes up to 25, looking closely, we can see that no one attended that many times – the maximum number of sessions attended was 24.

This graph is a fairly typical example of a so-called 'positively skew' distribution, in which the proportions with higher numbers of attendance fall off to the right. 'Skew' is referring to the distribution not being symmetrical. The mean (here 9.8) is indicated by the dotted vertical line and the median (6) by the dashed vertical line, and we can see that the mean is above the median, pulled up by the relatively small numbers of clients with many attendances.

Spread or distribution of data

The histogram gives us a detailed idea of the distribution of data. Real datasets show all sorts of distributions. For example, when a random number generator draws numbers for the many prizes in a lottery, they should have a flat, or uniform, distribution: every number that can be drawn should have an equal probability of being drawn. That is a very rare distribution to see in our field. Many of the variables that interest us - age, baseline measure score, anxieties about therapy - tend to have a single peak (that is the 'mode' or most frequently occurring value) and OM score distributions are often skewed and not symmetrical around their peak. Some distributions may be 'bimodal', as for the session count in Figure 5.8, which has two clear peaks each with its own most common value. Here, those two 'most common values' are 6 and 23, and it is clear that the data come from a stepped care service allowing either shorter therapies (up to six sessions) or longer therapies (up to 24 sessions). Strictly speaking, those data have only one mode: the most common value, which is 6 sessions. However, it is clear that there are the two subsets in the data, each with its own mode, so we talk of this as a bimodal distribution.

We have seen that the mean and the median are statistics describing 'central location'. What about describing the spread of the data? We met the SD, which is one general marker of spread, in the descriptions earlier in the chapter. Spread can also be described by the range, which is the difference between the highest score and the lowest.

Quartiles

Quartiles are another way to summarise data and the 'interquartile range' (IQR) is another measure of spread. The IQR is the distance between the 25th centile (the score such that 25% of the observed scores are smaller than this) and the 75th centile (the score such that 75% of the observed scores are smaller than this). The 25th and 75th centiles are described as the 'lower and upper quartiles'. They are called 'quartiles' as, along with the median (the score that bisects the distribution into two equal-sized halves), they separate the distribution into four parts. This brings us to boxplots.

Boxplots

A graph that you will find in many research papers and that helps us to visualise a distribution is the boxplot. The real strength of boxplots is for comparing groups, as we will show later, but here we will start with a boxplot of a single distribution. Figure 5.9 is a boxplot of exactly the same attendance data as we saw for the histogram in Figure 5.8 above. This boxplot has been annotated on the right to help you identify the parts of the plot.

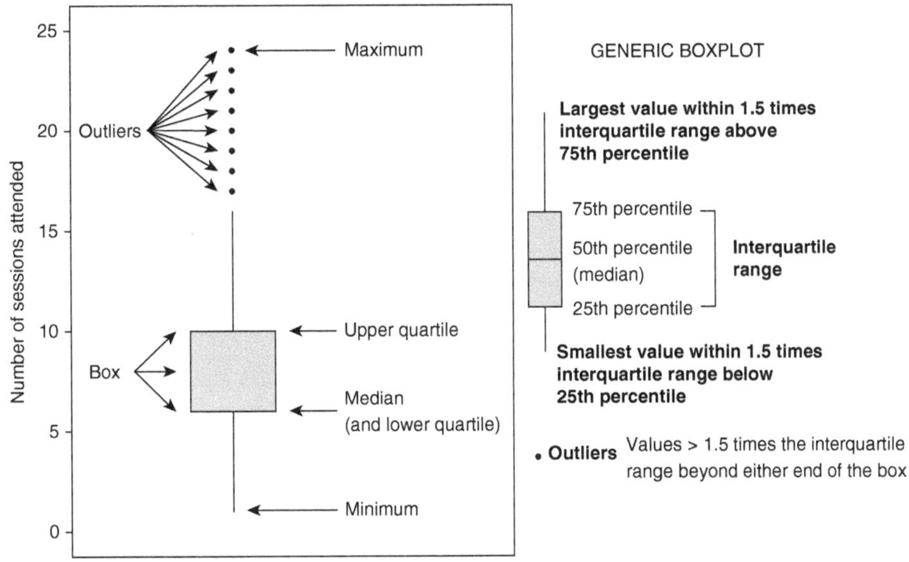

Figure 5.9 Boxplot of attendance

Looking on the left-hand side, you can see that the number of sessions attended is now on the y axis and the data are summarised by the *box* and *whiskers* and *dots*. The box describes the middle 50% of the data: the interquartile range we just introduced. That means that its lower edge is at the 'lower quartile' of the number of attendances: the score such that 25% of the observed scores are smaller than this. For this service that is 6. The upper edge of the box is the upper quartile of the score, such that 75% of the observed scores are smaller than this, here 10. There is a line, the belt of the box, through the median. Here, as would probably be true for real stepped care service data, the median is 6, the same as the lower quartile, so the belt and the bottom of the box are the same in this particular boxplot.

The distribution of attendances outside those central 50% are shown by whiskers (the lines pointing up and down from the box) and sometimes, as here, with points (dots) for 'outliers'. Where you see outliers, as here, you know that the distribution is 'heavy tailed'. This is about comparing the distribution of scores that would be expected in the 'Normal' or 'Gaussian' distribution, sometimes, helpfully, called the 'bell-shaped curve'. A heavy tailed distribution has more scores toward the top scores, or more towards the lower scores than you would expect in the Gaussian distribution. Whether distributions of scores were roughly Gaussian used to matter a lot as many statistical methods assume distributions are Gaussian but this is changing with new methods. We explain it here, as the marking of outliers is a standard part of boxplots.

For a single distribution, such as that above, the boxplot simplifies things and conveys less information than the histogram. However, when we want to compare more than two groups the histogram stops working and the boxplot comes into its own. Figure 5.10 shows the attendance count data as a grouped boxplot. Here the grouping separates the 6-session Well-Being Work (WBW) from the longer duration CBT and Counselling work, which is typical of the two 'steps' offered in a UK stepped care service. The plot further subdivides attendance by gender. As the vast majority of clients attending the WBW service attended the 6 sessions they were offered, the box is essentially squashed into a line, with those clients coming for 1, 2, 3, 4 or 5 sessions, as outlier points below it.

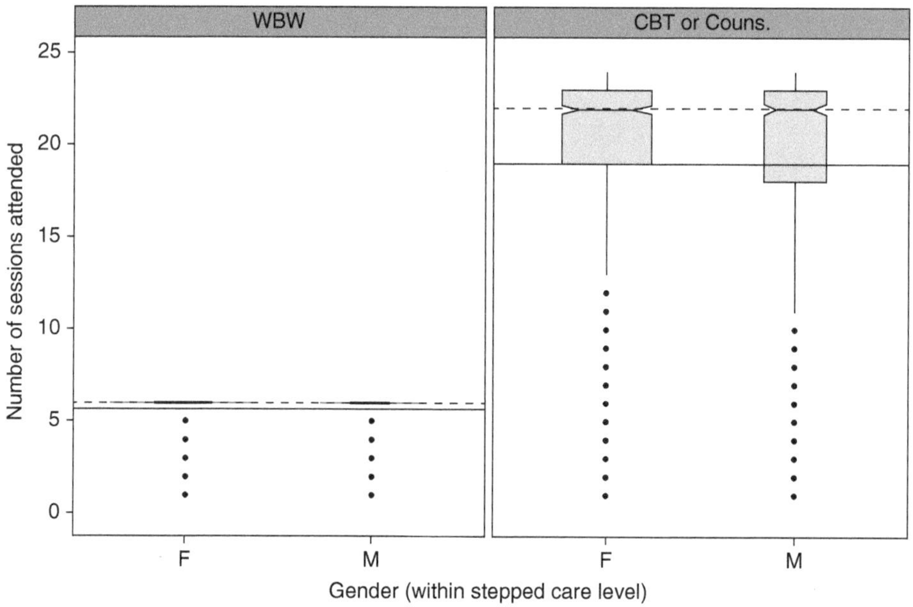

Figure 5.10 Grouped boxplot of attendance by gender

As we would expect, the attendance numbers are very different for the CBT/Counselling step, with the lower and upper quartiles well separated, so we can see a box. We can see that there is essentially no difference between the median attendance for men and women in either of the steps, although the lower quartile for the men is quite a bit lower than for the women. The widths of the boxes relate to the numbers in the groups, so we can see that there are somewhat more female than male clients in both the WBW and CBT/Counselling step.

You may have noticed the notches in the boxes for the CBT/Counselling step: how the boxes are pinched in above and below the belted waist that marks the median. These notches are a really valuable part of boxplots, but to understand their importance we need to keep building up our statistical knowledge. We will do this now and come back to what the notches can show us. To do all of this we are going to introduce a new larger dataset.

Using summary statistics to compare groups: estimation and 'tests'

As well as helping us to describe data, statistical methods allow us to ask how much of what we see is random or systematic. This brings us to another fundamental idea in statistics, that of 'significance': whether a finding is unlikely to be due to chance. There are a number of building blocks that help us to get to this 'significance' and we are going to take it one step at a time.

So, as the numbers of data points we have increase, whether because of aggregation across therapists or services, or even just for one practitioner, we start to be able to ask more questions of the data. Typical questions are: How do scores from one service compare with those from another? Are women's scores different from men's? Statistically, these questions are about comparing the central locations of score: Is the mean higher, or lower, in one service than another? Is the mean score for women higher, or lower, than for men?

When we ask whether differences between groups are random or systematic, the size of the group makes a huge difference to our ability to answer this. The bigger the sample, the more able you are to pick up small but nonetheless systematic differences, as random variation balances out across the larger numbers. Let us start with possible differences by gender and let us assume we have a large number of starting/baseline PHQ-9 scores from a service.

For a particular period of data collection, the 937 male clients had a mean starting PHQ score of 19.51 and the 2,008 female clients had a mean starting PHQ score of 19.82. OK, so there is a difference there of 0.31. We know that the median is another one of the statistics describing central location. Here the male median starting score is 19.3 and the female median is 19.78, giving a difference of 0.48. Those are pretty small differences on a score that can range from 0 to 27 but this is quite a large dataset, so do these differences suggest a small but systematic difference? We know that a grouped boxplot (Figure 5.11) will show us more about starting PHQ scores by gender.

We know the whiskers show the maximum and minimum scores in the two groups and both groups have scores ranging from 10 to 27, so there are clients of both genders scoring the maximum possible. The widths of the boxes confirm that there were more women than men. We know, from the introduction to boxplots above, that the boxes cover the interquartile range, that is the scores of the middle 50% of each group, so we can see that the lower quartile in both groups is similar, slightly lower for the women than the men, and we can see that the upper quartiles are again similar, slightly higher for the women than

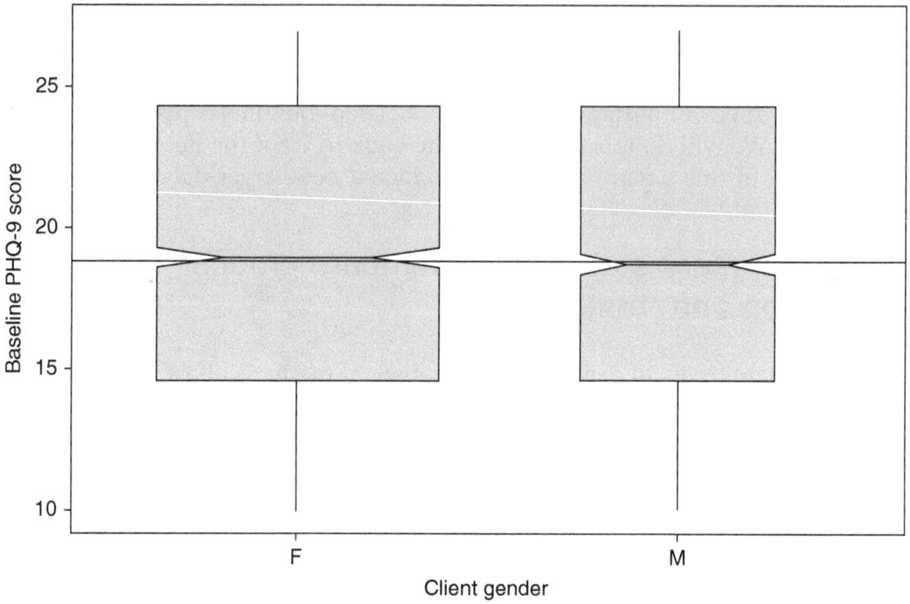

Figure 5.11 Boxplot of baseline PHQ-9 scores by gender

the men. The overall median starting PHQ score is shown by the horizontal line and, as we knew from the raw values above, the median for the women is slightly higher than that for the men.

Now we come back to those notches into the sides of the boxes. By 'notches' we are referring to the upper and lower point where the boxplot starts to nip-in to the belted waist: the median. These are going to help us to decide if the small difference in starting PHQ scores we are seeing in the medians might be systematic.

Estimation and confidence intervals

In this section we are going to introduce the idea of confidence intervals (CI) as part of our journey to decide whether a difference is systematic or not. These 'notches' or waists we have seen in the boxplots show the *95% confidence interval for the median*. What does this mean?

If we keep taking sets of data from similar services, say every three months, then even if the median of all the data together is, say, 19.6, it is very unlikely that any of our individual datasets will have exactly that median. This is to be expected for any data. For example, if we roll dice, we will not get the same scores each time we roll them, nor will be we get the same total scores each time we add up quite a large number of rolls.

We are talking about datasets, whereas statisticians talk about 'samples' and about 'populations': each time we roll, say, 10 dice, it is a sample from the potentially infinite population of all possible rolls of those dice. When we have datasets from services, this idea of them being samples from a population gives us useful tools with which to analyse our data.

Whether we have random or non-randomly created datasets, whether of rolled dice or of attendances at a service, their medians *will* vary: if sampling is random, these are termed 'sampling vagaries'. It sounds like a problem but, mathematically, it gives us a vital procedure, a generic and invaluable tool. Simplifying a little, a 95% confidence interval can be generated mathematically around any observed statistic from any sample. In this example, the observed statistic is the location of the waist, the median score for each service. The notch tells us the that *if only sampling vagaries were operating*, for 95% of samples each of the same size as these (i.e. 2,008 for the women and 937 for the men), the observed medians would lie within the notch. Confidence intervals tell us about the precision of estimation of a population value from a sample statistic. Or, put another way, confidence intervals tell us how precisely our figures represent a given population from a sample statistic.

We can see that the notch is tighter (either side of the median) for the women than for the men. This is an inexorable fact about *all* data collection: if other things are unchanged, the more data we have, the more precise is our estimate of the value for the hypothetical population; here the estimate of the female population median is more precise than for the men.

We should go back to 'populations': what are they? Sometimes there is a known population of known size - for example, the women and men on the electoral register. More often, as in our example, it is hypothetical: the notional population if the service kept running and accruing data for some years.

However, the key thing about this sample-from-population is that it tells us about 'generalisability': the population that matters for us is the collection of people to whom we are hoping our sample findings generalise.

Coming back to our data, the fact that the median for the whole sample - that horizontal reference line across both boxplots - lies within the notches for each gender, in formal terms - that it lies within the confidence interval for the median for each gender - tells us that this difference could easily have arisen by chance and is not likely to indicate a systematic difference. In chapter 8 we will give an example where the line does not fall within the notches and where there is a significant finding. The following section is going to give you a bit more background about this idea and introduces the other main way to explore whether or not effects are likely to be systematic rather than random.

Tests: *p* values, significance and hypothesis testing

After confidence intervals, hypothesis testing is our last statistical method to explore whether things are random or systematic. If you read quantitative reports, understanding both confidence intervals and hypothesis testing will cover all you will need for this.

In the example above, we have been looking at the difference in the median of the scores by gender and we have seen that using confidence intervals tells us the precision of estimation of the medians for each gender.

Furthermore, it showed us that, given the sample sizes, the estimation was not so precise that the small gender difference can confidently be said to be systematic: we cannot say that a gender difference is likely to be generalisable to the wider population.

Another way of addressing this is 'hypothesis testing'. To understand this, we need to know about the 'null hypothesis' as significance testing starts out with this. Here, the null hypothesis is that there is no difference in the PHQ scores between *all* men and *all* women who could come to this service. The null hypothesis is a model about the population.

This statistical method is famously associated with the Guinness brewery, where William Gosset developed statistical ways of measuring how confident the managers might be that one yeast (say) worked better than another. Gosset explained to the managers that there was no 100% certain way to decide from an experiment whether changing from one yeast to another would improve fermentation. He went on to explain that every time Guinness did an experiment, they would get slightly different results by 'sampling vagaries' as the realities of brewing, like those of therapies, are not exact.

However, the statistical methods he developed meant that he could tell them what the risk was that an apparent advantage of one yeast over another was just down to chance. The managers decided that they would adopt the new yeast if that risk was as low as, or lower than, one in 20, a 5% chance.

That convention has continued and has become a criterion of statistical significance. Where differences between samples are as unlikely as one in 20 to have happened by chance, i.e. if the null hypothesis were correct about the population, then the differences are designated 'statistically significant'. This is usually expressed as '$p < .05$', i.e. that the probability of this difference occurring by chance is less than 5%. Applying Gosset's *t*-test to our data will test the 'null hypothesis' that there is no difference in the PHQ scores of all men and all women who could come to this service. Looking at the data from this sample, we find that this probability is 0.15, which is above 0.05, so, by long-hallowed traditions going back to that Guinness brewery, we 'accept the null hypothesis' and conclude that the data do not support there being a systematic difference by gender.

Summary

In this chapter we have taken you through a series of methodologies that help you understand how analysis of change data in ROM can be summarised, visualised and presented. We have moved from the simple representation of tables and plots to building up more complex plots and graphical representations that also tell you something about reliable change and clinically significant change. We finished by exploring the underlying concepts of hypothesis and significance testing and showed how these can also be represented graphically using boxplots. For some, this will have been a hard read, but we hope that it gives you the tools to digest and critically examine the data that you come across in research reports.

Although we used relatively simple examples, these methods can apply for many more complex and interesting questions that we might have about outcomes in psychological therapies. For example, if we think clinically about the factors which might meaningfully affect change scores, we might want to consider factors such as: having had therapy before, being on medication, diagnosis, social status, employment status, etc. In principle, as data accumulate to provide large enough datasets, one can explore whether there are systematic differences between these things. In the long run, therapists wanting to conduct thorough statistical exploration of questions about predictors will need to:

1. Link up with other practitioners and pool data to get big enough datasets to comment confidently on particular relationships between variables and to agree what relationships to explore.
2. Link up with a statistician or statistically trained and experienced practitioner who can advise on *how* to explore those relationships.
3. Think through with that person exactly which relationships are to be analysed (and how), *before* looking at the data.
4. And only then feed the data into a statistical package with the work being done or supervised by that statistician/practitioner who can really understand the best way to input and analyse the data.

This chapter has tried not to over-simplify the handling of change and outcome data as the dangers of over-simplification are huge. We have tried to show some of the issues in words, pictures and numbers because we think that all those approaches, i.e. narrative, graphical and numerical analyses, are necessary and complementary. The different approaches are also important because it is well established that people differ in which presentations of data they find easiest to comprehend. The next three chapters will build on this chapter by looking at more specific situations: how to set up a routine evaluation and the difference of doing that as a service or a lone practitioner. Any collection of data with thoughtful analyses based on the ideas and the tools provided here really can add something to the narrative reporting more familiar in counselling and psychotherapy.

Note

Colour images available on the authors website

PART III

EVALUATION – APPLYING OUTCOME MEASURES IN PRACTICE

6

Planning an outcomes exploration: design and be SMART

This chapter sets out the things you need to think about when planning an outcome or change exploration. Two things can cripple this kind of project: design faults and not recognising the logistic issues. We will describe a process that will help you to find a design that is 'workable' for your situation. This starts with the absolutely key question of: What do you want to tell, to whom? When you know this, you can begin to plan. We will start with design and then move to pragmatics using SMART: **S**pecific, **M**easurable, **A**chievable, **R**elevant and **T**ime-framed. Of course, design and logistics are interwoven: there is no point in a design which is not achievable.

So, design starts with what do you want to tell to whom, works through the related issues of the data you will need to collect and how you will analyse it, and must never ignore how you will communicate it. Therapy data, both quantitative and qualitative, can be little better than random noise if they are not embedded in wise planning, analysis and reporting.

What do you want to tell and to whom?

An outcomes evaluation tells a story about change, whether this is a single therapy or across many clients. The design that is best for your purposes gives structure to this story and is inextricably linked to your setting and your audience: what do you want to find out about, and who do you want to tell about it?

Who is your audience? This might be your clients and potential clients. It is often your peers, whether locally or generally, and it may be non-clinician audiences such as managers, commissioners or wider stakeholders and policy makers. As ever, different audiences find different data and analyses persuasive. Potential clients probably find narratives and simple summaries of your change data helpful. Depending on modality and research orientation, fellow therapists may want more exploration of diversity of change and possible contributory factors. Stakeholders often want to see that we are reflective and trying to improve efficiency (usually with tabulated data!).

You need a question or questions you want to explore. Perhaps you have a particular idea about your work with older people? Perhaps you want to identify your outliers - people you do particularly well or poorly with - and learn from them? Maybe you want to compare how your aggregated change data compare with colleagues? Keep your audience in mind and remember that the more you hope to tell everything to everyone the more you doom your work to fail.

Fit your design to your audience

In planning your design, remember that you may need to communicate your findings to a number of different audiences and the type of information you want to share will vary. Personalised change and qualitative narratives about change might be most useful with individual clients, while aggregated, nomothetic change data might be most informative for commissioners. No single type of information can ever give a complete picture of what has happened across a therapy or therapies. Like a good book or painting, all data collection selects and simplifies from a more complex reality. This is as true for narrative case reporting as for quantitative questionnaire reports. We return to these issues in Chapters 9 and 10.

Here we will look at how different audiences may want different OMs.

What outcome or change matters to your clients?

Ironically, this is probably the most avoided question when designing evaluations. As therapists, we tend focus on what *we* think matters. 'User involvement' balances that.

Many clients start therapy with significant distress and want information about the likelihood of short-term improvement, but most also want an idea of whether improvement will be sustained. However, the very beginning phase of therapy, or even just completing an OM (Chapter 3), can change the ways clients view themselves and their difficulties. Hence clients' aims may change quite quickly. We need to remember that this question of what outcome matters is a multi-layered one and easily over-simplified.

Different clients want different changes. Well-being measures may be fine for mild anxiety or depression but not for clients presenting with utter despair and thoughts of suicide. Clients presenting a fourth time, who have benefitted previously from medication and therapies, may now seek different things from the first time they sought help. General measures should try to cover most clients' foci, but none can cover everyone's. Specific measures are very good for specific problems, but those may address the problems of a minority of all clients. These issues show how a client-generated measure such as PSYCHLOPS or the Personal Questionnaire (Chapter 4) allow a fit to each client's interests.

What outcome or change matters to you the therapist (and why)?

Very often there is some congruence between therapist and client about what should change. However, the congruence is not always perfect. Nomothetic measures are inevitably a compromise, with an approximate fit to the aims of therapists or clients (Chapter 2). By definition, a nomothetic measure is designed to be acceptable to as many people as possible, making it an imperfect fit for any one individual. Using both a nomothetic measure and a client-generated measure can give a useful double focus, ensuring that views of individual clients are not overlooked.

One key issue is of modality. We touched on this in Chapter 4 (Table 4.1) and will come back to it in Chapter 7. Modalities differ in how much congruence they expect between client and therapist constructions of problems and desired outcomes. For example, the theory of analytic and psychodynamic therapists suggests that some of the difficulties the client brings to therapy will be out of their conscious awareness. Thus, the aims of a psychoanalytic therapist may be to change things of which the client is unconscious. Hence there cannot be a simple congruence of their aims. In that modality, what a client may see as their goals is probably expected to change over time. Many family/systemic therapists also have concerns about simply privileging individual clients' views rather than looking at how the whole family functions, although they would probably not talk about the unconscious in explaining this. Within the solution-focused school of systemic (and individual) therapy, the focus on problems is avoided and the work of the therapy is to find solutions by escaping the trap of focusing on the problem. In this example, outcomes may be solutions being found rather than the reduction of symptoms. Many arts therapies believe that it is the emergence or (re)release of a generic creativity and spontaneity that will provide long-term change, not focal problem change.

Ostensibly, nomothetic measures like the CORE-OM or OQ-45 will be more congruent with CBT or interpersonal/humanistic therapies than with analytic, arts or systemic therapies. However, nomothetic OMs can still be in tension with these modalities. Many CBT therapies are tightly problem-focused, meaning that CBT therapists sometimes mistrust general OMs, preferring specific measures. Interpersonal, person-centred or humanistic therapies often have a very particular emphasis on the individual, which can mean that they are also uncomfortable with nomothetic measures that relate to symptoms or well-being.

Despite all this, there is a strong concordance across therapies, and across clients, about what constitutes a positive or problem state. Thinking 'it is not what I would really like to use but it is not completely unacceptable to me' may be a good enough aspiration when faced with the design question 'What measure do I want to use?'.

What outcome or change matters to your external audience?

By 'external audience', we mean groups outside therapy professions, particularly managers, commissioners, epidemiologists and politicians. Some of these audiences have very particular interests. 'Specific' and 'Relevant' in SMART may mean we use measures that speak to these audiences, particularly Quality of Life (QoL) measures (Chapter 4), when we are trying give data that are persuasive to those who can increase or reduce funding to a service. Of course, such actors may already have chosen your primary OMs for you.

Audience and power relationships

As you will have noticed, one of our concerns is that your audience may have a power relationship with you and this may cause challenges. Managers and commissioners will be concerned with value for money and politicians should be interested in the aggregation of data across multiple practitioners, potentially on a huge scale. Such foci are generally not those of therapists. However, there is little to be gained from resisting change or becoming locked into resentful disempowerment. We hope at least one of the strategies below will help you to recover confidence when sharing data with external audiences and help you to build meaningful conversations with them.

What data analyses are persuasive to your audience?

Not only are different OMs differently persuasive to different audiences, but different analyses of data also vary in persuasive power, depending on your audience. Most clients will want their own data to be simple, some will prefer plots, others the numbers. All will want a narrative to explain the data and its presentation.

Fellow therapists are often more receptive if quantitative change reports are complemented with some narrative case reporting. Psychiatrists and psychologists tend to expect quantitative data, but also to expect that it will be presented with statistical analyses. Both professions still over-value 'statistical tests' and p values (Chapter 5), but that is changing. Managers and commissioners are often anxious about statistics, which were rarely included in their training, and generally prefer tables and plots, often against referential values, i.e. data from other sources. However, they may also be quite receptive to free-text client feedback and stories of clients' experiences of services in their own words. Presenting the same data using different analyses for different audiences may markedly change the responses to the data. It is worth finding sympathetic collaborators to give guidance on what will be persuasive and to help you write reports. Partners for such collaborations come from diverse places, so be creative, opportunistic and open-minded. They might include charities with specific interests or trainee professionals (for example, counsellors, psychiatrists and psychologists) who may need the experience of carrying out 'service evaluation', 'audit' or even 'research'. Fostering such relationships may be a rich and synergistic way to get data analysed and reports written.

Good design

Once you have your focus and audience you need a design. Data on their own can feel useful, but they rarely tell a useful story unless they have been collected within a design. A design links the questions you want to explore to a plan of analyses, and through those to the communication of the findings. Statisticians often talk about 'DAPs' (Data Analysis Plans), which start from the aims and must have a design that will make use of your data to address your aims. Designs making persuasive use of OM data include the following:

1. Single case reports or case series. Changes in OM scores provide an added context to basically qualitative, narrative work.
2. '$n = 1$' quantitative change studies. These overlap with Embedded Change Management (ECM), in which sessional/weekly OM change data are used to change the therapy delivered. We will come back to this in Chapter 9.
3. Collated OM data, simply summarising change. These typically mean change or percentages achieving reliable and/or clinically significant change. These data are most informative if compared with other data.
4. Collated OM data that identify potentially 'informative outliers'. These might be most improved clients, deteriorated clients, and most erratic change trajectories, which are then analysed qualitatively.
5. Collated OM data seeking statistical relationships, e.g. baseline predictors of change.
6. Collated data describing change over time, such as 'sudden gains', 'on track' and 'off track' trajectories.
7. Collated OM data seeking dynamic predictors of change, e.g. 'process/outcome studies' linking change in OM scores to events and processes within the therapy or, a much neglected issue, linking change to external events.

Each of these designs could merit a book this size (and many of them have books of many sizes, if not always focused on therapy and OM change). We absolutely do not want to discourage you from collecting your own data, but some of those designs really do need expertise and experience and we encourage you to find collaborators and, ideally, people with pertinent research experience if your questions take you towards some of these designs. If such support is unavailable, which is still too often the case, categories 1, 3 and 4 above are the best for you.

SMART design

The SMART checklist helps to keep design realistic. As we have already noted, **Specific** and **Relevant** apply to your choice of OM, but all of SMART applies to design issues: focus, data (OM), analyses and communication.

Specific is about being clear and concise about what it is you want to measure and specificities may vary with audience. To an audience more in the "medical" model these might be symptoms and diagnoses; to a CBT audience these might be thoughts and behaviours; for a health economic or political audience this might be "quality of life" against costs.

Measurable. We have already that said you almost certainly should not create your own measure. Use an existing OM that has demonstrated its robustness, for example through the reliability and validity checks we introduced in Chapter 3, that were ideally found with similar clients to yours.

Achievable is crucial. No real data are complete or uncomplicated, but a dataset that is largely or systematically missing data can give no generalisable findings. If you are lucky enough to have a clinic administrator who might give out measures, that will not work if s/he finishes at 3 pm and your clinic works until 6 pm. There is no point expecting all service practitioners to participate in an evaluation if you have not committed time to ensure that they are on board with the project (non-participation is at least as important with professionals as with clients). These may sound like obvious points, but we know from painful experience that if these issues are not considered early and honestly, they create irretrievable problems.

Relevant is obvious. Simple examples include not using an eating disorders measure in a generic therapy service unless you really are only interested in a few of the clients. Likewise, measuring psychological mindedness as a possible predictor of change will not persuade your commissioner to keep funding your work. S/he only wants to know about opt-out rates and change, no matter how much you may think psychological mindedness affects those things.

Time-framed. Setting realistic time objectives is essential. If your service is under threat of closure and you want to present some data on client satisfaction, you need to work fast. On the other hand, we know that one of the biggest limitations of many studies is the short follow-up time frames that are reported. So, if you *can* build in longer term follow-up, you will be adding really valuable data to what currently exist. Most people underestimate the time frame needed to collect enough data to give a meaningful story. That takes us into sample size and design.

Sample size and designs: pre-post designs

Pre-post designs are historically the most frequently used designs and do what they say: they analyse measures from before and after an intervention, usually from the first and last sessions. The big challenge is whether enough of your clients complete the measures at the last session. In many routine services, opting-out and non-completion at the last session reduce those with pre-post data to under 50% of those who start therapy.

Sessional data

That problem has contributed to a huge shift throughout the 21st Century from collecting pre-post data to sessional data. One clear advantage of collecting data weekly or sessionally (not always the same) is that we can see trajectories of change as well as collecting far more clients with first–last change data.

Numbers of clients, of sessions and of therapy endings

Most people think that statistical questions - questions about whether something is random or systematic - can get clear answers with relatively small amounts of data, say from five to 30 clients. As we saw in Chapter 5, statisticians refer to 'precision of estimation' and we almost never get much precision from such small numbers. We might think a coin is biased if we toss four heads in a row. In fact, the likelihood of getting the same face in four tosses of a coin is one in eight, which is hardly very improbable and well below the Guinness model of statistical significance (Chapter 5).

It can be frustrating that quantitative data on small numbers of clients will inevitably seem 'thin' compared to rich clinical recollection of the conversations and interactions you had with those clients. However, even quite thin numeric data can reassure commissioners that the practitioner or service is confident enough to be transparent and evaluate outcomes. Done well, mixed methods (i.e. methods combining quantitative and qualitative data and analyses) are very powerful. The quantitative data can give an overview of change and its diversity, and the qualitative data, for example vignettes illustrating both good outcomes and problems, connects the numbers back to human beings and avoids the idea that simple numbers mean therapy is simple.

Too often such service reports only show a tentative willingness to share quantitative data and use poor quantitative methods and no qualitative method at all. Reports with thin and poorly analysed quantitative data, say pre-post change data from 30 clients out of 78 who came for therapy, with some cherry-picked, appreciative users' comments, can look good once or twice, but it will not stand up to critique from commissioners or funding bodies. It is unsurprising that such reports are produced given the 'austerity' pressures on services, but we hope we can start to move beyond this. This will require new conversations and change from practitioners/services *and* from managers/commissioners, and we return to this in Chapter 10.

Quantitative, qualitative and mixed data and methods

The design issue here concerns the pros and cons of quantitative and qualitative methods and how best to combine them. Aggregated quantitative OM data give a picture of typical changes for a client group and, if there is sufficient data, can suggest whether these changes are systematic or random. But ROM data cannot reveal or dissect the subtleties of therapies. Qualitative data can explore the complex interactive and collaborative processes of therapy and describe important and unusual events, but these can rarely be generalised from a specific instance, a single case or small group of cases. The more quantitative data you have, the more you can look at relationships between your variables. This means that high throughput, short duration therapies lend themselves to quantitative outcomes analyses even for a single therapist, whereas therapists working with longer-term therapies will have much to gain from building combined datasets through sharing their quantitative data. There is a strong tradition of longer-term practitioners sharing case reports, which can throw light on processes within and across sessions, but these can be very misleading if generalised to other cases. A shift towards longer-term practitioners collecting and sharing routine data has huge potential to change that.

Design options are shaped by logistics and must be SMART ambitions, not magical, aspirations. However, *any* therapist or service can collect useful OM data that will be useful both to their understanding of their work but often also useful to others, external to their practice or service.

Design and issues of confidentiality and ethics

Sharing data brings us to a huge practicality: basic human rights, specifically rights to confidentiality. Clients always have the legal right to request access to their own data and, where services are publicly funded, any member of the public in the UK will have rights under the Freedom of Information (FoI) Act to ask reasonable questions of a public service that might include analyses of, or even provision of, aggregated anonymous data. The proviso here is that sharing must not leak the identity of any client nor involve 'disproportionate effort' to provide it.

Where data are purely nomothetic and quantitative, publishing analyses will almost never breach confidentiality if data are handled properly. By contrast, qualitative data, even very simple data such as the problems volunteered by a client on PSYCHLOPS (Chapter 4), might leak identity, and great care must be taken to tell clients how such data will be handled and confidentiality protected.

Technically, confidentiality is compromised if the individual client might recognise themselves from the data reported, so having a record of informed consent to collect these sorts of data is good practice. Most clients, if they feel the use of the data is congruent with what had been explained and feel confident that no one else would recognise them or judge them, will agree to their data being collated even if they can recognise their own data. However, extreme care should be used in reporting qualitative data to external audiences as even individual nuances of expression may identify someone to a third party. Signed consent for this is wise, if not vital, and explanations must be sufficiently detailed that an individual is fully informed about how the data will be stored, anonymised and reported.

These ethical and legal issues may preclude some desirable designs and options for data collection and reporting, and they must always be thought through carefully before starting any data collection. However, the principles are not complicated and many ethically viable designs remain.

When not to measure!

Moving on from qualitative measures and mixed methods, and some of the ethical considerations about data collection, we believe there are two situations when it is justified *not* to use OMs at all: (1) where no viable OMs exist, and (2) where the client's use of the OM may be so wide of the aims of the therapy as to be misleading. Within these, we see three main situations in which no viable OM exists, and two situations in which self-report data might become misleading.

1a) If the OM does not exist in the client's language or if their language/culture is such that the OM does not make sense to them. Many OMs have few or no translations from the original language of construction and some translations may not be fit for purpose. Sometimes a questionnaire may seem to be a valid self-report measure in the host language, say to commissioners, but may not be for the client. Even 'depression', in the way we understand it in the UK, much of Europe and North America, may not be a universal phenomenon. For example, the term was rarely used in Japan until the late 1990s. Many of the items of OMs designed in Europe or North America may make no real sense to often severely traumatised refugees from other countries.

1b) Another situation where self-report measures may not be appropriate is when someone's cognitive abilities are not suited for typical self-report, e.g. for some children, some people with learning disabilities, autistic spectrum and other neuro-diversity, people with neurological injury, and people with dementia. At the moment there is a lack of adequate exploration of how to seek informative self-report from these groups, and little work on what might be best to use in the absence of self-report. These are areas ripe for investigation. A specific example might include whether affect laden questionnaires are appropriate for people with 'autistic spectrum' presentations.

1c/2a) Where clients are psychiatrically 'psychotic', i.e. experiencing delusions and/or hallucinations that interfere with their ability to, or willingness to, describe their own experience to others. This would include situations where the person is operating in another frame of reference such that both nomothetic and client-generated self-report may be unhelpful and may generate or exacerbate anxiety about the intentions of the therapist.

2b) Finally, there are situations where practitioners are working with a client group, for example, some forensic and some anorexic clients, when the aims held by the therapist may be very different from those of the clients. Forensic clients suffering anti-social personality disorder may have less investment in an increase in empathy than their therapists, and almost by definition, most anorexic clients have less commitment to weight gain than their therapists. In such cases, self-report measures may not be useful for change. In these settings it may still be valuable to use self-report measures and to look back at them with the client at the end of therapy, when the clients' and therapists' views may have converged. It may also be possible to find measures that are acceptable to the client and not irrelevant in the eyes of the therapists and audiences for the data. For example, alliance measures and complex measures like repertory grids or qualitative interviews used for OM purposes may be useful.

Making the best of imposed OMs

We will finish by coming back to some suggestions when you have to work with imposed OM data. By this, we are referring to measures decided by service managers or imposed, for example, in the NHS dataset.

1. Don't be an ostrich, try to connect with other people's focus!

Managers and commissioners are trying to maximise gains with limited resources. Often the OMs they seek or impose are not perfectly congruent with what practitioners and/or clients want. However, they are rarely so discrepant as to be worthless. Most therapies do help clients and QoL and symptom change measures will very rarely fail to show this. Work with managers and commissioners to remind them that data collection costs time and money, but accept that optimising the completeness and integrity of your data can markedly improve the perceptions of a service.

It is almost always possible to find constructive ways to use imposed OM data. For example, being able to show that particular groups of clients contribute to more of the negative outcomes is useful information for a service and may help to argue for more specialist input for those groups. Being willing to explore differences in change within your service, or findings that are discrepant with those from other services, is more useful than just asserting that all your outcomes are excellent. Exploring the less good outcomes can address important questions: Do you have high social deprivation in your client group? Are there more ethnic minority clients than the national referential rate and is this reflected in your staff team? If not, could poor outcomes be linked to lack of inter-cultural awareness? What are the implications of this for engaging with your local community and potentially improving outcomes? How do your initial scores compare with the national scores?

An emphasis on 'cost offset' may enable you to push for longer-term outcome data. There is emerging evidence that some longer-term therapies facilitate change with clients that sustains better over time than that from shorter therapies. This will only be understood in cost terms if you collect data over longer periods of time. Related questions might be: Does the intervention you are using give cost savings in other services? Is there evidence that a longer intervention may stop re-referrals?

So, although they do have weaknesses, the extensive data collection systems in many healthcare systems, particularly in the NHS, may offer real opportunities to discover, at an anonymous and aggregated level, what the long-term outcomes in our clients are.

2. Try to piggy-back your interests onto imposed data collection!

It may be possible to use the infrastructure of the larger data collections systems to ask questions that concern and interest you. For example, collecting simple alliance or client satisfaction data alongside the imposed OM data can lead you to more understanding of opting-out. Combining this with focus groups with clients to discuss what inhibits attendance or use of the therapy can form a rich, mixed dataset that managers and commissioners may come to respect.

3. Meet poor evidence with better evidence, not just with contempt: look for allies!

This is really a twist on the last strategy. Being prepared to learn more about research, so that you are in a stronger position to give a critique of the data and the analyses, is a healthy option. We will return to this discussion in Chapter 10.

Summary

This chapter underlined that having a good design and being practical are both vital to get useful ROM data. The design links what data you collect to what you want to do with it, and what you want to say to whom through what analyses. No one measure and no one design fits all services and all audiences, so design carefully, and get help from colleagues, users and, if you can, researchers. Equally, no data collection that is not practical will produce good data, so be SMART!

7

Outcome measurement for individual practitioners

In this chapter, we explore ways an individual practitioner might use OM in their practice. Even thinking about collecting OM data and what it might tell you can open up interesting questions you had not previously considered. However, quantitative change data from any individual practitioner can be thin if the numbers of clients they see are not large. Any practitioner, regardless of modality and caseload, will learn more from change measures about their clients' experiences if they link up with others in similar practices. A key message in this chapter will be to try to find others working similarly and to develop ideas together.

Because what you can discover is so strongly determined by the numbers of clients seen, we are using two very contrasting fictional therapists and imagine that most readers' work will lie between these extremes. For each case study, we have suggested possible questions to ask of the OM data that we think are realistic. Our questions are not exhaustive - they could not be - but they illustrate options. As you read through the two case studies, think about how your work differs from these practitioners and about how questions that interest you might also differ.

Short-term practitioner

Christine sees her work as eclectic, drawing on trainings she has had both in existential therapy and in CBT as well as courses and reading she has done on solution-focused therapy and positive psychology. She believes her skills are not in longer-term work, so she only offers six sessions within a year and often works with a model of a single-session therapeutic consultation. She does encourage clients to return after a year if they want a booster/refresher session or if they have new things they want to address. She thinks that about 30% come back once, 10% twice and only about 5% come back a third time. Christine knows these are rough estimates and that she would like to have more accurate figures and to understand more about when people come back and why. However, she wants to start by understanding more about the first episodes and has some questions that interest her (see Box 7.1).

Box 7.1 Christine's research questions

1. Do her clients show improvement, as assessed on a self-report measure?
2. Are there specific identifiable factors that predict improvement?
3. As her clients can come for one to six sessions in these first episodes, does OM change according to how many sessions the client attends?
4. Are second and later episodes of therapy different from initial ones?

Christine would like to know what happens after people finish, so she decides to start inviting people, when they first contact her, to fill in online the same two short questionnaires she uses on paper within sessions. She also decides to start sending follow-up emails inviting clients to do the same online questionnaires at one, two and three months after finishing. Thinking about one aspect of client confidentiality, Christine words these emails so that clients could claim it was a request to participate in some research unconnected with therapy if anyone else saw the email.

What features of a change measure or measures should Christine consider?

Christine wanted a measure whose items covered the typical issues clients bring to therapy, but she also wanted at least some items to be positive. She likes to watch how clients complete the measures and reads through the online completions before her first meeting with clients. She talks with the client about their ratings and asks if the measures felt congruent with the problems that brought the client for therapy.

She chose to use the CORE-10, which has no licence fees and two positively cued items ('I have felt able to cope when things go wrong' and 'I have felt I have someone to turn to for support when needed'). In addition, as Christine is interested in health economic evaluations, she also chooses the ReQoL-10, which has six positively cued items. She decides she falls under 'Individual

Medical Practices' for the ReQoL, so she does not have to pay for it. Both questionnaires ask about the last week. At the start of each session, she asks people to complete them and often discusses clients' responses during the session. Addressing consent, Christine explains to clients that she is hoping to share information from the questionnaires with other practitioners, perhaps through publications that anyone could read, but explains that no one but her will ever know the identities of clients.

Christine's second question (see Box 7.1) concerns things that predict change. She feels that there are likely to be differences relating to age, chronicity of problems and social situation, so she makes a note of these variables, including social and employment status, and starts to construct a table to collect all the relevant data (Table 7.1). Even if you work very differently from her, what changes might you advise to that table? If you did something similar what would your table look like?

Table 7.1 Christine's data

When	What	Christine's notes
Receiving the referral	ID code	
	Date	Crucial!
	Self-referral	
	Other referrer	Build a list, can categorise later
	Reason for referral/presenting problem	Build a list, can categorise later
	Previous therapy	
	Previous therapy notes	Build a list, can categorise later
	Did make contact before but didn't come	
	Seen before, returning	Make note of how many times and dates
	All item responses on measures	Online completion at time of contact. Recording all items allows check on internal reliability
At first meeting	Gender	
	Age	
	Employment status	Use official statistics categories
	First language not English	
	Needs interpreter	
	Physical health issues	Build a list, can categorise later
	Agreed contact with GP	Any notes about this
	Social status	Categorise using census categories

When	What	Christine's notes
	Dependents	Build a list, can categorise later
	Medication	Particularly psychotropic medication but any other too. Categorise later with help from a psychiatrist.
	DNA/cancelled/late	Categorise into DNA: Y/N, cancelled Y/N & how late
	Number of sessions planned	Christine sometimes works one session at a time for up to her maximum of six but also sometimes agrees a number at assessment
	All item responses on measures	
	DNA/cancelled/late	
	Any changes in life situation since referral	Build a list, can categorise later
	Coping level	
	DNA/cancelled/late	
	Date	
After each meeting	Changes in life situation	Build a list, can categorise later
	Notes on session	May categorise as process variables later
	Date planned for next meeting	
	All item responses on measures	
	Date	
Online follow-up	All item responses on measures	
	Any comment in free text area	Build a list, can categorise later

Box 7.2 What questions would you ask about Christine's work and data?

Even if your work is very different from Christine's, you might want to pause here and think. Do her questions (Box 7.1, above) interest you? What else might you explore in her situation? How do you think she should handle the data she will accumulate?

Her third question is about differences in change on her measures, possibly relating to the number of sessions. She realises that she will have a pattern of data like that in Table 7.2.

Table 7.2 Christine's data by session

Category	First contact	First meeting	2nd session	3rd session	4th session	5th session	6th session	One month later	Two months later	Three months later
Never came	±									
One session	±	+						±	±	±
Two sessions	±	+	+					±	±	±
Three sessions	±	+	+	+				±	±	±
Four sessions	±	+	+	+	+			±	±	±
Five sessions	±	+	+	+	+	+		±	±	±
Six sessions	±	+	+	+	+	+	+	±	±	±

It is very rare for a client to refuse to complete a measure in a session, but Christine soon finds that some of her clients do not complete the online forms she sends them at referral and at the three follow-up points, hence the '±' in Table 7.2.

Having had advice from fellow practitioners, Christine realises she also needs to get more methodological advice. She discovers that her registering body has a research network that is keen to link up with practitioners. Through those contacts, she finds a sociologist and a statistician interested in what she is proposing. Both agree to help her on condition of co-authorship on papers. They agree to meet to think about how to use the data.

At the first meeting, Christine shares her questions (see Box 7.1). To help her colleagues to understand how her practice works and what data are likely to be available Christine talks through what she thinks are the common trajectories with her clients. Christine has been using paper forms in sessions for some months, but has not previously collected online data from them before the first meeting. However, her sense is that almost no one who attends describes having got worse immediately prior to the first session and she imagines this may be the relief of having sought help.

Thinking about the first meeting, some clients agree that one consultation, with the option to return if they feel they need it, is enough, and some others agree to return. A small number agree to more sessions but cancel or simply do not attend. She is not sure that any of them will fill in online follow-up questionnaires.

For those who do come back for an agreed second session, she says that scores can change in all three possible directions (better, worse or the same) by this second session. Christine thinks that between session 2 and 3 is a point when some clients terminate: some agree with her that they want and need longer-term work and Christine often helps them to find another practitioner; some clients are already feeling better and decide to terminate; a very small number just disconnect.

Across subsequent sessions Christine says, on the limited data she has already, that data mostly show fairly stable scores, although she suspects that the few with whom she agrees six sessions are a bit different and are more ambivalent about the ending. She feels that some are confident about things having improved, but others are sad or anxious about the ending and she knows that some feel that they have not been able to make the changes they had hoped for. She thinks that as the numbers build up, these reactions will be evident in their scores. She does not know what data from the emailed invitation to complete follow-up questionnaires will show, but hopes gains will be sustained. Christine does not yet feel she can predict what the outcomes of "returners" (about 30%) will show when she starts to collect more follow up data.

Christine and her colleagues start to think about how to use the data that will accumulate. Thinking about the quality of the data, they agree to check the internal reliability of each measure and will also look at the convergent validity correlation between the two measures (Chapter 3). They expect that reliability and convergent validity will be strong as there seems to be a fit between the design of the measures and Christine's client group. They agree that if correlation between the measures is very high then it would be possible to drop one of the two.

Turning from the psychometrics to the change scores, they start with Christine's first question about the majority of her clients improving and agree that it is sensible to plot the distributions of scores at each time point, and, for those who have scores at multiple points, to look at the distributions of the scores at each time point and at change in scores between points. They agree that means are the obvious way to summarise these scores and that the best comparison with other reported data will be on change from first session to last session (whichever is the last session). However, they all agree that for the clients who do complete follow-up questionnaires online, that follow-up data are very important in describing whether, or how much, change is sustained and even whether there may be continuing improvements for some clients. Considering individual clients, they agree that the Reliable Change Index and Clinically Significant Change parameters (Chapter 5) are useful and familiar to both practitioners and researchers, so, like mean change, can probably be compared with data from other services.

They note that many clients may not complete the follow-up questionnaires so this rate must be considered and reported.

They then turn to Christine's question about possible predictors and observe that Christine sees these as two sets of variables: some reflecting ambivalence about change but others she sees as more 'fixed', such as gender, age, social situation, etc. She sees DNAs (do not attends), cancellation and lateness as the markers of ambivalence. The statistician points out that with many variables, and several different time points at which to consider change, it is important to select a few things that interest them most. They agree that gender must always be considered, as should age, although they do not expect age to be a strong predictor of change. They feel that previous therapy, use of psychotropic medication and Christine's indicators of ambivalence are their key predictors. The statistician notes these as planned foci that will be at the heart of her Data Analysis Plan (DAP). Having pre-specified foci allows for the use of statistics to say how likely it is that any effects found are not just chance ones. She explains that the DAP will also include exploring for strong effects of other variables on the accumulating change data but will recognise that some of those may be chance findings.

Finally, they think about Christine's last two questions: about the numbers of sessions and about returning for more therapy. The statistician explains that the number of sessions is another 'predictor', although a rather complicated and interesting one. The statistician explains that they should look to see whether number of sessions is strongly associated with the other predictors, such as 'Does Christine regularly plan more sessions with people on medication than those who are not on medication? Do men more often fail to attend planned sessions than women?' They agree that, again, this is complicated and they will revisit this after looking at the impacts of session counts. She says that the question about second and later episodes of therapy is somewhat similar and they will start by looking at whether any of their variables, including change in the first episode, appear to be systematically associated with returning.

The three of them agree to meet again a month later, after the statistician has written up the DAP and shown the likely precision they can expect to have for their focal analyses after one, two and three years, assuming that Christine's current throughput of clients stays fairly stable. At that meeting Christine is disappointed to realise how slowly she will get very clear findings. However, they agree that there is little published about this kind of exploration of clinical practice so what she is doing really adds to the knowledge base. They agree with Christine that she will collect the planned data for three months as a 'pathfinder' phase, to sort out any emerging challenges and to have the reassurance of seeing data accumulating and some simple summaries by the statistician to encourage her that it will be worth continuing to collect the data. They agree that, after that pathfinding work, she will contact her training organisation and registration body to see if the

DAP and her experiences will encourage other practitioners to join her in the same or a similar data collection exercise. They are starting to form a Practice Research Network (PRN).

Longer-term practitioner

Jan's modality is psychodynamic so for her the crux of the work is in the analytic unconscious. She believes that clients' problems may come from conflicts that the client is not immediately aware of and with which she and her clients will work over months or years. Jan believes that self-report questionnaires cannot penetrate the processes that keep unconscious mental life out of consciousness. However, she feels that most of her clients are broadly sympathetic with Freud's idea that a successful therapy leaves someone much more able to make choices to 'love and work' and she thinks that a number of short self-report measures can tap that, and measure some of the problems that clients report. Jan does not want measures to be embedded in the therapy where she feels they will be distracting. She is aware that about a third of her clients opt out of therapy before, to her mind, the work can really help, usually within 2–8 weeks of starting. She decides that she has three main areas of interest that OMs could illuminate (see Box 7.3).

Box 7.3 Jan's research questions

1. Do those who stay long enough generally show improvements on OMs?
2. Do gender, initial questionnaire score or early changes in scores predict clients terminating early?
3. Is change in longer-term clients linked to changes – perhaps improvements – in lateness and number of cancelled or non-attended sessions (DNAs)?

Jan knows she needs allies for this work. She will need practitioners who work in similar ways to join her if they are to accrue a useful amount of data in a reasonable time. She also wants non-therapist allies to get other perspectives on her ideas and particularly someone with statistical expertise to tell her how many colleagues she should aim to get on board. She teams up with a friend, Sarah, who has had therapy and brings 'user experience'. Sarah works in social sciences in a local university. They decide that the challenges are:

1. How can Jan explain the questionnaires to clients without putting too much emphasis on the data collection in ways that might distract from the therapy?

2. How often should she ask clients to complete measures?
3. How can they look at whether there is any association between change on measures and other activities, such as opting out of therapy early, attendance, etc.?
4. How many colleagues does Jan need to join in data collection?

Box 7.4 What questions would you ask about Jan's work and data?

Even if your work is very different from Jan's, what do you think about her questions and how she might explore them? What features of a change measure should Jan consider?

They decide that Jan will start a pathfinding process to see how the data collection goes as soon as they have had advice from a statistician. That will enable her to explain the possible collaboration to fellow therapists. They agree that she will use some time in her first meeting with new clients to talk about taking part, saying something like this:

> *I am a therapist, not a researcher, however, I am working with a researcher and fellow therapists to see if we can build a better understanding of how people's problems and issues change over time. Questionnaires are a simplified but useful indicator of this and they have the advantage of not giving any information about someone's identity. I invite all my clients to fill in a questionnaire which I will give you every month at the same time as I give you your invoice. There will be an envelope for you to return it in that only has a code number on it. I like to concentrate on our work not the measures while we work together, so I give the unopened envelope to my colleague who will never know anything that could possibly identify you. You are free to take part or not and can withdraw at any time if you wish: participation will not affect your therapy.*

Jan and Sarah discuss measures with the provisos that they must be free, acceptable to clients and fit with the kinds of problems that bring clients to therapy. They agree on the CORE-OM. By giving the questionnaire at the same time as giving clients their invoices Jan makes sure that she remembers the questionnaires. When she prepares the questionnaire and envelope, she puts the clients' code numbers in a spreadsheet where she records the accumulating data on lateness and cancellation/DNA, along with a simple record of assessment data. Jan also has a separate dataset where she notes other information after each session and at the end of therapy (Table 7.3).

Table 7.3 Jan's data

What	Jan's notes
Assessment information	
Date	
Gender	
Age	
Employment status	Use official statistics categories
Social status	Categorise using census categories
Medication	Particularly psychotropic medication but any other too. Categorise later with help from a psychiatrist.
DNA/cancelled/late	Categorise into DNA: Y/N, cancelled Y/N & how late
After each session	
Date	
DNA/cancelled/late/left early	
Major changes in situation since last session	Build a list, can categorise later
Notes on session	May categorise as process variables later
After termination	
Date of last session Date finalised termination	Particularly with earlier terminations Jan says these are often different when a client opts out with little discussion
Reasons given for termination	
Any major life changes across the therapy	
Comments on therapy process	Very simple categories Jan thinks will stabilise after the first year

Sarah will collate the questionnaire data and thinks that they can analyse it annually to address the questions that she and Jan discussed. They also need statistical advice and they arrange to talk with a statistician in Sarah's university about those challenges.

At their first meeting with the statistician (Sian), they are surprised that she starts with words not numbers and underlines some words in Jan's list of questions:

1. Do those who stay long enough generally show improvements on OMs?
2. Do gender, initial questionnaire score, or early changes in scores predict clients terminating early?

3. Is change in longer-term clients linked to changes – perhaps improvements – in lateness and number of cancelled or non-attended sessions (DNAs)?

Sian comments that it was a relief that they did not come asking for tests and to prove things. She explains that those words 'test' and 'prove' are only relevant when the design behind the data collection is suitable and that many study designs are actually descriptive and exploratory but very valuable nonetheless. She says that Jan's words are loose to a statistician but fit with exploratory, descriptive statistical methods and she agrees that drawing graphs summarising the accumulating data will be informative. Sian also suggests that using confidence intervals to show how precisely Jan's data will address her questions and using some 'tests' in an exploratory manner will also help. She suggests rephrasing Jan's questions as:

1. Do OM scores of clients 'staying long enough' show improvements rather than staying the same as the months go by?
2. Do the data suggest there are systematic associations between gender, initial questionnaire score, or early changes in scores and clients terminating early?
3. Is that change systematically associated with reduction in lateness and in number of cancelled or non-attended sessions (DNAs)?

They agree the rephrasing is clear and that Jan is not asking to 'prove' that anything she finds will be true for future clients of hers, or for other therapists, although she believes it will help her to understand and explain more about her style of work to prospective clients. She also believes it may raise questions of interest to other therapists and clients. Jan acknowledges that with data only from her clients it will take a long time to get much precision in the findings and says she hopes that she will be able to find colleagues who would collect similar data. She thinks that through personal contacts and organisations she will find between 10 and 30 fellow therapists willing to collaborate and explains that she is planning a pathfinder year of data collection on her own first. She says she knows she needs statistical advice about the numbers.

Sian agrees that the plan sounds sensible but continues to look at the language. She points to 'staying longer' and asks if Jan can tighten that up, explaining that any ambiguity about definitions dramatically reduces the utility of data. Jan says she tells most clients at the first meeting that she thinks it takes at least a year before people start to see sustainable changes. She says that many who do not stay that long do get some useful experiences and positive change so she would define 'staying longer' as staying more than three months even if it is not reaching her preferred one-year point.

Sian then asks how many clients does Jan have at any one time and how long do the therapies last? Jan says she generally has about 20 clients in therapy and that she thinks that about a third who start do not stay three months. She admits that she does not have precise numbers but thinks that about half stay between one and three years. Using this, Sian says that assuming all of Jan's slots are full, she would see around 21 new clients each year. Jan thinks that about one of these will stop coming before one month and so have no initial change score. About another six will stop before three months, and the rest (about 14) will be longer-term clients.

Sian explains that they can look at the precision Jan will have for her findings and at how the precision increases as the number of other therapists contributing their data increases, assuming similar durations of therapies for the colleagues.

Sian explains that for Jan's first question about OM scores improving over time for clients 'staying long enough' that obviously 'improving' means that the slope of scores against time will be downwards and that if all clients participate, Jan will have 200 to 240 completed questionnaires per year and about 80 or 90 of these will be from the nine new 'staying longer' clients (as she will not have data for her existing clients). Clearly, as Jan keeps collecting data, the longest duration over which she has data for any one client will grow, and the number of completed questionnaires from 'staying longer' clients will grow. Sian says that scores are continuous variables which helps with precision and that they should be able to look at each client's slope of score against time and look at how many show a downward slope that seems systematic, and unlikely to have arisen by chance. They agree that it will also be important to see how many clients ultimately show clinically significant improvement, i.e. move from a typical clinical score to a typical non-clinical one. Jan says that in her experience symptom/problem change in the first months can be quite erratic and that clients who eventually seem to do very well often have early exacerbation of problems. She says that some also become anxious near termination. Sian explains that with the substantial numbers of scores per client, as the numbers of therapists, clients and years accumulate, it becomes statistically possible to look at change in different phases of a client's therapy, although this uses a relatively new statistical method.

Turning to Jan's second question about predictors of staying longer, Sian says they can take gender as an example and hears that the gender ratio in Jan's clientele is about 60:40 female:male and she points out that the 60:40 split means that on average 13 of the 21 new clients will be female and eight male. If the issue of interest, 'staying longer', means more than three months and on average about two-thirds stay that long, then the question about gender and staying longer is 'how big a difference does gender make?' If there is no difference between gender and staying longer, then the nearest fit to those proportions is that five of the eight men and nine of the 13 women will stay longer than three months (Table 7.4).

Table 7.4 Breakdown of Jan's clients by gender and duration of therapy

	Early	Later
Women	4	9
Men	3	5

Sian says that statisticians, like gamblers, think in terms of 'odds ratios' (see Chapter 5 for an introduction to odds ratios), i.e. the ratio of the short stayers to the long stayers among the men compared to the ratio for the women: the ratio of the odds. For the nearest fit to 60:40 F:M and 2:1 long:short for 21 clients, the numbers (3/5) / (4/9) gives an odds ratio of 1.35. An odds ratio of 1 means no difference between the groups. Here, the odds ratio of 1.35 is the nearest fit to an odds ratio of 1 given the sample of 21 clients and the 60:40 gender ratio and assuming that there is no effect of gender on staying longer.

Sian says that if Jan can get other therapists to join her, and assuming each has a similar practice to Jan, i.e. assuming that each contributes 21 clients per year and each has a 60:40 F:M ratio and a 2:1 long:short stay ratio, then Sian can tell them how the pooled data will become more and more precise. She illustrates this to Jan with a graph (Figure 7.1).

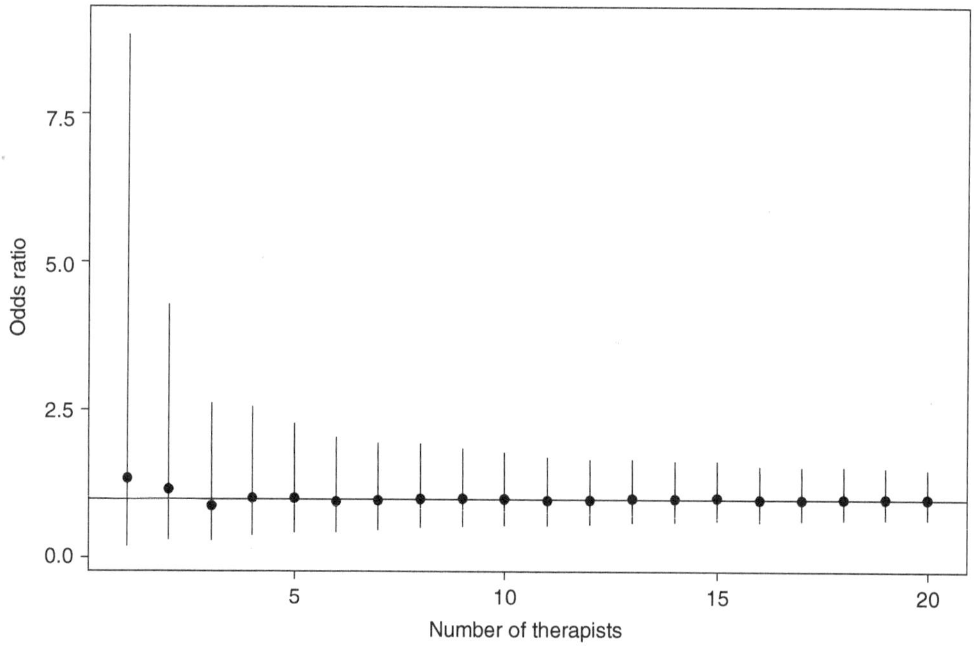

Figure 7.1 Odds ratio of effect of gender on therapy duration: null population model

Sian explains that the x axis is the increasing number of therapists and the y axis is the odds ratio. She explains that the horizontal reference line shows the null odds ratio of 1 that marks no effect of gender. She shows that the observed odds ratio - the points - fluctuate with each added therapist and stabilise fairly rapidly close to 1.0. She adds that what is really important are the vertical lines through each point marking the 95% confidence intervals (Chapter 5) for the odds ratio. She points out how these get tighter and tighter as the number of therapists goes up. The 95% CI with just Jan's own 21 clients is from .12 to 8.9, which includes a huge range of possible gender effects, whereas with 19 other therapists the interval tightens to .65 to 1.5. Even then, moderate effects of gender are still clearly possible.

Sian then says that she can show them a model of the same thing but based on some different assumptions. She assumes that the ratio of short to long for women remains 1:2 (i.e. a rate of 1 in 3) but changes her model to assume that men are twice as likely as women not to 'stay longer'. In this case, the rate for men is 2 in 3 and the ratio for men of shorter:longer is 2:1, so the odds ratio for the women staying longer is (2/1) / (1/2) = 4. Those of us who rarely gamble may have to re-read the arithmetic to convince ourselves that doubling of the rate of shorter stays for the men, a 'relative risk' of 2, takes the odds ratio to 4, not 2. Readers used to betting and thinking about odds will find this unsurprising. Sian explains that the mathematics of odds ratios are easier than for relative risks so most research papers will report odds ratios, which is why she (and we) use them here. Sian shows how adding therapists works for this population odds ratio (Figure 7.2). Note the different numbers on the y axis.

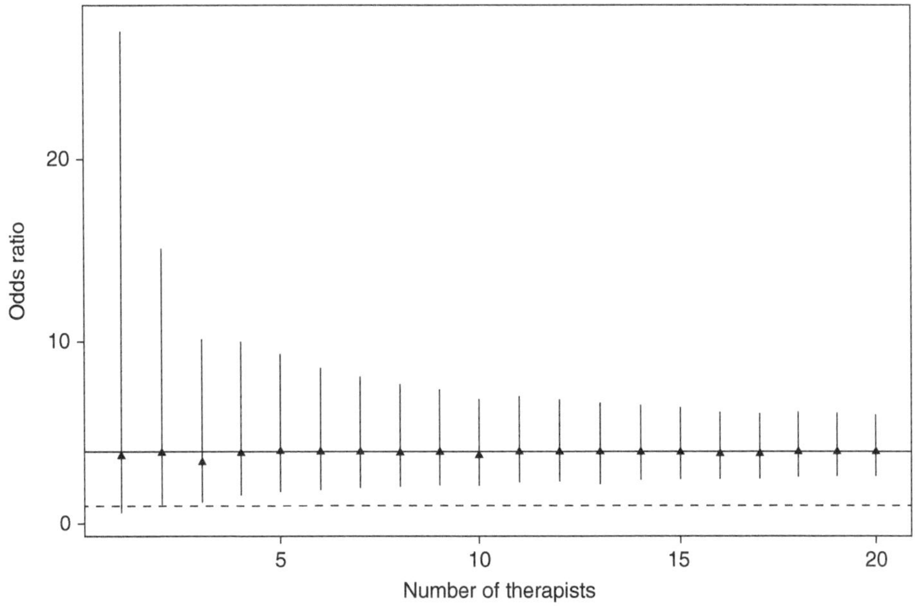

Figure 7.2 Odds ratio of effect of gender on therapy duration: non-null population model

She says that the principles of the plot are the same except that the solid horizontal reference line is now on 4, again marking the population odds ratio, but that she has left the dashed reference line on the null model odds ratio of 1. Then she shows them the two models combined (Figure 7.3).

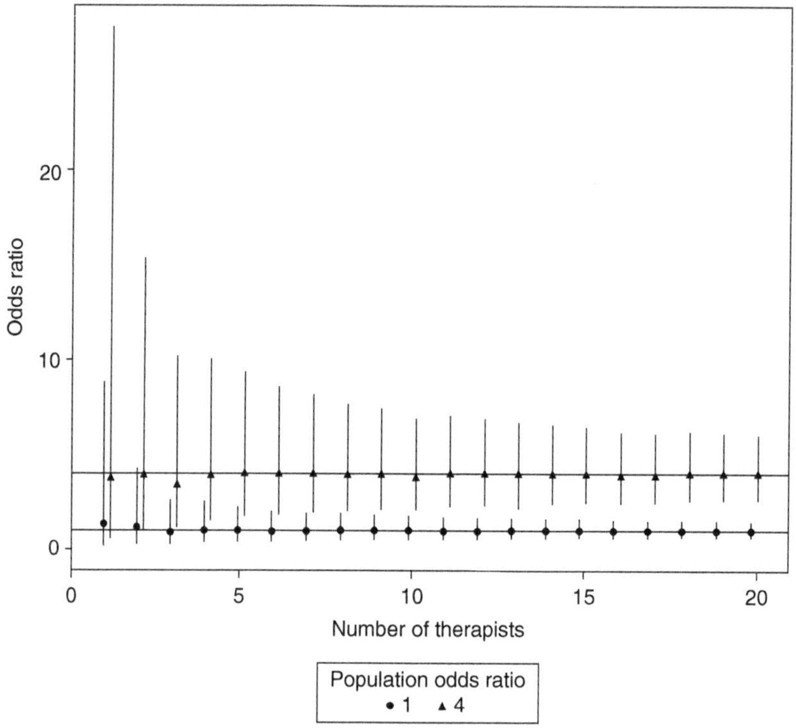

Figure 7.3 Odds ratio of effect of gender on therapy duration: both population models

She explains that she has nudged the plots either side of the actual numbers of therapists so that the confidence intervals do not overwrite each other. She says that they can see that the precision of estimation improves with increasing numbers of therapists participating for both models, but that they can also see that even with three therapists (i.e. 63 clients), the confidence intervals for each model no longer intersect the other model's odds ratio, so Jan and her collaborators would be starting to get a useful precision to detect fairly large differences between men and women, such as a doubling in the proportion of clients staying longer. She says that statisticians often talk about this as the 'statistical power' of a design. This refers to the projected number of clients that would be needed to detect an effect – here, the effect of gender on duration of stay.

The general rule that larger numbers of clients will always give tighter confidence intervals and greater precision is obvious: more data means less uncertainty because of randomness, and the same applies to statistical power: it always goes up with increased numbers. Sian explains that although precision and power always improve with more client data, the improvement is faster for some questions of interest than for others. She says that in general questions about counts, such as how many are 'staying longer', gain precision less rapidly with increasing numbers than do questions about continuous values, such as OM scores.

Finally, they look at Jan's question about whether longer-term improvement is related to reduced rates of DNAs and lateness. Sian says that this has three parts. The first is about improvement in OM scores over time. The second is about some clients reducing DNAs and lateness over time, and the third is any relationship between those two. Jan says that in her experience some clients have very low rates of DNAs and lateness, which means that they cannot change that much over time but that most of these clients will show improvement over time. She thinks there is a separate group of clients who have quite high rates of DNAs and lateness at the beginning of therapy, and for most of these those rates come down with time and she expects their questionnaire scores would show improvement following this. Sian says that without knowing rough numbers of DNAs and lateness, it really is impossible for her to predict the likely precision of estimation that Jan will get.

Sian suggests that Jan should aim to persuade as many other therapists as possible to join her, ideally the 30 that Jan thought she might find. Only after that number have been collecting data for a year or more will they be in a position to look at this question and see how much more data would be needed to be moderately confident of showing any systematic relationships.

Client numbers and comparing with summary data from other practitioners

These two case studies were of explorations of ROM data from individual practitioners. Christine sees so many clients she may get answers to her questions over a year or two without others joining her in data collection but much more will be learned if others join her. As Jan works for longer periods with clients, it is essential that others join her if they are to learn more.

As well as data sharing, another option to understand more about your own data is comparison with summary statistics from others, generally from publications and reports. Of course, to be meaningful there must be some similarities between your data and the other data. This could be reporting using similar demographic data, minimally gender and age. Comparisons are strongest if the same OM has been used by you and in the reported data. However, even if different OMs have been used, it may still be possible to look at numbers achieving reliable and clinically significant change and there are ways to compare the 'effect sizes' of mean change.

One challenge when comparing your data with other summarised data could be summarised as the apparently paradoxical: 'mean change may or may not be the difference between mean scores'. Where the mean baseline and termination scores are reported for the clients who completed the measures on both occasions, then the difference between the two means will be exactly the same as the mean change for those people. However, all therapists or services will have clients opting out of therapy and often you will find that baseline scores are reported for all who started in therapy (or came for assessment) and that this is a much larger number of clients than the number for whom the mean termination score is reported. In that situation, the difference between the means will not be the same as the mean difference for those doing both measures. When reporting your own pre/post data, make sure you report the baseline scores for all your clients who started treatment *and* the score for the generally smaller number for whom you also have a termination score and hence a change score. If collaborating with another clinician or service, make sure they do the same. Now you can compare your data with theirs, asking several interwoven questions:

1. Are my baseline scores for all clients completing the baseline measures similar to theirs? How different are my mean baseline scores from theirs? Does the 95% confidence interval around my mean of all baseline scores embrace their mean and vice versa? The two confidence intervals tell you how precisely your mean baseline score and theirs were estimated from your samples.
2. Are attrition rates (non-completion of therapy and/or final OMs) similar? Again, confidence intervals for the rates help you to decide if any difference may be systematic.
3. Are mean change scores for those who do complete both measures similar? Again, confidence intervals should be used.

People tend to read too much into data/differences that look large but come from small samples. You may feel excited that your change score *mean* is much bigger than a published one, as this appears to imply greater improvement (or you may be dashed if the comparison is the other way around), but be careful: if your mean is from only five clients and the published one from 10, then even really quite huge differences could have arisen by these sampling vagaries, as we discussed in Chapter 5. Even one more client, either in your data or in the data that had been reported, might have changed things considerably. This is a thread throughout this book from Chapter 5, where we first introduced confidence intervals, and we hope you can see how they help to avoid that problem.

Of course, such comparisons get more interesting if a number of services or clinicians have shared data. When comparing with multiple other sets of reported data a great tool for comparison is the forest plot of confidence intervals (see Chapter 5 and Chapter 8).

Even if there are systematic differences, we should not leap to assume that where there are differences in mean change, for example in comparisons of therapy duration or modality, that you can conclude one setting is better than another. There is an understandable tendency to jump to such conclusions, but it is important to remember that the difference in duration, or modality, may not be the only difference between the client groups. For example, one set of clients may be coming for their first therapy, the other may be of clients who have had between one and five previous therapies.

Comparing data is a qualitative and narrative skill as well as a quantitative and statistical one. Our cautionary notes about using confidence intervals are quantitative, but it is just as important to see that comparing findings creates a narrative which will note geographical and organisational differences between the data sources. It will return to the quantitative to note demographic differences to the extent that the same demographic variables have been collected. It will go back to qualitative if commenting that collection of different variables may throw light on the interests of the therapists. In this narrative reviewing of the data, it is vital to watch for differences in how variables are categorised. For example, ethnicity categories can vary across reports and can be radically different in different countries. Similarly, descriptions about gender identity or about partnership status categories often differ in small but significant ways. All this links to the need for as clear a picture as possible of the durations and processes of the therapies.

Comparing ROM with controlled trial data

One perhaps surprising cautionary note is about comparing ROM data with data from therapy research trials. Trial data may not be comparable with your data because many trials will have excluded a large number of potential clients who do not meet strict study criteria, thus reducing generalisability. Delivery of the therapy will have been standardised, with strong encouragement to clients not to opt out early and to complete the OM.

Sadly, OM data from trials is far more easily available than ROM data from services. Trials receive research funding (which may well match the budget of a routine service seeing 100 times as many clients) and the funding rightly insists on, and underwrites the costs of, the publication of findings. As usual, following the physical health sector example, the research trial industry has spawned a further funded industry of 'systematic reviews' and 'meta-analyses' (analyses of analyses) comparing findings from different trials. The focus was entirely on aggregating answers to the 'which is better?' question. However, since the beginning of the 21st century, meta-analyses have become more sophisticated and tools have been developed that allow the exploration of questions other than 'which is better?'. These allow 'subgroup' analyses – results for men to be separated from those of women, for example – and can explore whether the size of the trial or its methodological sophistication relate to the outcome.

ROM data is of course about routine clients and routine outcomes and does not exclude clients unless they refuse to complete OMs, so the diversity of participants in ROM reports tends to be large. Similarly, services' ROM data will reflect that there is much more diversity in interventions offered in routine services than is true in trials. The complexity of ROM data contributes to the relative slow development of methods to compare ROM data and trial data. However, the main reasons why this is developing slowly are that many therapists have avoided collecting ROM data but also that ROM data receives little research status or funding. These frustrations and differences between ROM and trial data should not stop us comparing the two, but the challenges should not be underestimated and there is a need for new attitudes of constructive sharing of findings that we return to in Chapter 10.

Collaborating to share anonymised data: 'little data' vs 'big data'

In the modern world of 'big data', everything we have been discussing until now is 'little data'. This should not be read as a weakness - there are great strengths to comparisons conducted by sharing small datasets, and repeatedly in this book we encourage you to look for colleagues with whom you could share your research interests. Meeting regularly in a group like this can be really supportive, but it can also help to keep your motivation going when things seem daunting. The group members do not have to have the same aim, and it is probably going to be a healthier and more creative group if they do not. There is more to learn if members discuss their different interests and ideas for ROM and research and think together about what measures they might use and how to share data. At the beginning, you could perhaps look at recently published research papers and digest them together. These groups are sometimes referred to as Practice Research Networks (PRNs) and we urge you to encourage training and registering organisations to provide the infrastructure to support such groups and (properly anonymised) data sharing.

Of course, there are advantages to having bigger datasets, or 'big data'. Large, pooled datasets allow explorations that might have been meaningless with smaller ones. The larger the datasets the greater their statistical power to detect relationships and the more precisely they can estimate effects. This gain in precision means it becomes possible to explore the interactive effects of multiple variables on change. We saw this in Jan's case study: change in OM scores against dynamic predictors of changes in DNA and in lateness rates require aggregation of quite a lot of data, something that is simply impossible with the data from single practitioners.

This power can be seductive, and analyses of large datasets should still start with the same graphical and tabular summaries that we have introduced in the book so far. Beyond those methods, data analysts can employ powerful statistical methods, such as 'multi-level modelling', 'machine learning' and 'artificial intelligence', which are currently very alien to clinicians and to all but a tiny subset of therapy researchers. Sometimes these more technical approaches are bandied around as if they are the answer to all methodological challenges. They may have the power to improve on the very crude 'league tables' that are often used politically to judge work in the public sector, or they may be just as misleading: these methods are still in their infancy and given far too much credence and far too little real testing. It is vital that large datasets are shaped by the questions that practitioners and clients want to explore and not simply by researchers and politicians.

Summary

We hope our two fictional therapists have helped you to think about your own work and what OM data collection, and what data analysis, might help you to learn and share. As so often in this book, we have underlined collaboration and we have looked specifically at comparing your own data, or your service's or network's data, with other ROM data and data from trials. We finished by trying to give you a balanced assessment of 'big data', which took us back to the importance of our getting involved with OM as therapists and practitioners, and not leaving it to researchers or politicians.

8

Service-level change and outcome measurement

Many services in the UK National Health Service (NHS) already have service evaluation based on ROM data and this is also increasingly true of health services in other countries. Throughout the first decades of the 21st century, the use of OMs in such services has increasingly shaped thinking by politicians, commissioners and managers, which makes it useful to understand how OM data can be used in such services even if you do not work in one or expect to do so.

Sadly, many of these systems lack genuine input from local practitioners, and adopt naïvely 'managerialist' designs that can alienate practitioners. These programmes are expensive and we believe it is tragic that they rarely optimise the real involvement of local practitioners, service users, referrers and commissioners. Equally sadly, there are countless organisations that do not yet collect routine change data at all. That leaves huge scope for services to make better use of ROM data.

This chapter will use a large fictional service to act as a case study. The simulation data have been designed to illustrate particular questions and features of what ROM can offer and does not pretend to represent any real service. If you work in a service, do think about the similarities and differences of your own service. If you do not work in such a service, remember that much of what we will discuss is also applicable to smaller-scale ventures and collaborations between single-handed practitioners. Finally, do remember that these systems, good or bad, have huge political impact.

A multi-practitioner service – case study

This fictional service supplies therapists to 130 primary care health centres serving about 300,000 people. The area has a very mixed geography and diverse demography, including small rural villages and towns, and a large town that is struggling with the collapse of the heavy industry and which includes areas of significant diversity as well as of social deprivation.

The service employs about 250 therapists at any one time. Many therapists work on a part-time basis, a few work entirely within one location, but most work in more than one location. Some of the therapists have worked in the service for up to 30 years and have seen many changes in service philosophy and delivery. However, most came into the service in the last 10 years during a period of expansion. This newer group has high turnover, tending to change roles within a period of two years. There is substantial diversity in therapists' trainings, which range from under a year of formal training to five or more. Some therapists have had multiple trainings in different modalities. All can claim to be trained in, and delivering, one or more of the therapies approved by the NHS.

The majority of the therapies are individual and short term, and the service is organised in a 'stepped care' model. These 'steps' are 1 = 'watchful waiting', 2 = short-term therapy (up to six sessions) and 3 = longer-term therapy (maximum 24 sessions). The majority of work is classed as CBT. However, there is also couples' and family therapy, psychodynamic counselling and short-term psychodynamic therapies. The group therapy that exists is for psycho-education and support and creates a substantial throughput of clients since these groups include some large, short-term groups with up to 30 people attending.

The service is commissioned by the local health authority and 'austerity' means the service is always pressured to deliver approved therapies to more clients for less money.

Routine data collection has a varied history locally, with some therapists having pioneered first/last session data collection as much as 25 years earlier. Sessional data collection is now mandatory and must include the 'NHS/IAPT minimum dataset', including the PHQ-9, GAD-7 and WSAS (Work and Social Adjustment Scales) (see Chapter 4 for more on these). Although all practitioners do collect the data, there is a very marked range of sympathy with this.

All data are entered into a single, NHS-mandated, data collection system that produces the routine reports for commissioners and for the national oversight system. It also allows managers, supervisors and individual therapists to see individual client data and aggregated data tables and plots, and there is an expectation that each practitioner's data are inspected in both line management and clinical supervision sessions.

Looking at a large dataset

The newly appointed director of the service believes that the service is making limited use of the vast amount of data and is keen to improve this. She realises that engaging the therapists is crucial as many are mistrustful of the measures and only collect them reluctantly, whereas others support the use of sessional measures but feel frustrated by how little information they can get out of the system.

Before we go further ...

Box 8.1 Aspects to consider for large datasets

1. What might you think of doing in the director's position? Imagine yourself on a 'user involvement group', what might you want to see the service do?
2. Imagine that you are one of the therapists who mistrusts the data. What are your concerns? How might you feel on hearing the new director's wishes to expand and improve the use of the data?
3. Now imagine that you are a therapist located towards the other end of the pro-/anti-measures dimension. What are your thoughts on hearing there is scope to use the data in new ways? What projects might you want to do?

We can make some real-world assumptions for this fictional service:

1. No new data are going to be collected as this would involve additional resources of time and money that are not available.
2. NHS politics mean any changes in data collection need to be approved by commissioners. However, they are unlikely to object as long as they continue to receive their current reports.
3. If you had unlimited time for data analysis, there are a nearly infinite number of things you could do with such an enormous dataset: selectivity is needed.

Having invited you to note your own ideas about how to proceed, below we elaborate on some of our thoughts.

After accepting those constraints, the first issue we would address is the pro-/anti-measures dimension among the practitioners. Good data never come from people who hate or fear the data collection. Neither do they come from those who are over-ambitious or idealising of data. We suspect that a short conversation with senior staff will rapidly identify a few different views:

1. 'The data is just a means of trying to attack the service, to get rid of people or force them to work even harder, instead of providing what patients need.'
2. 'The data is irrelevant: it is not measuring what matters as *that* cannot be captured by stupid tick box forms.'
3. 'The data collection intrudes on my work with clients.'
4. 'This was imposed on us and we are fed up with being imposed upon.' This may include those who liked the measures they were using previously and who may not be 'anti-measures', just 'anti-these-measures'.

If the director wants to collect really good data, she will have to address these issues. Our own answers to each of these views would be as follows:

1. 'That's absolutely not my intention. I would expect supervision and management to flag up and address the rare poor performance in the service. There will be differences between therapists' OM change data, but such differences will be far smaller than the effects of differences between clients and between practices and referrers. In the longer term, OM data might tell us about who seems to work best with which clients, but OM data will not be used to "get rid of people" or to force them into more activity. The aim is for the data to help us explore where we work most effectively, but that will only come when we understand our data much better than we do now.'
2. 'Of course, the subtlety and skill of what therapists do is complex and not measured by such forms, but almost all clients want to change in the directions that suggest improvement on these measures. I'm not saying these measures are perfect, and I know they are like knowing the weight of your carrots rather than how they taste. However, this really *is* information that helps our conversations with clients and commissioners. In that sense, they are simply not "stupid, tick box forms".'
3. 'Only a tiny number of patients have said they do not like these measures. There may be something we can do to minimise the impact and I am open to ideas about how we could do that.'
4. 'I agree that these have been imposed on us and I sympathise. However, they have been with us for a long time now and are unlikely to go away. There may be better things we can do as a service and there are certainly worse ones. As we must collect the data, I want us to understand what it can tell us and how we can use it better than what we do now.'

Strategic approaches to managing data collection and analysis in services

So, anyone managing a service where there are inevitably diverse viewpoints about the pros and cons of data collection has a dual task: firstly, to engage practitioners; and secondly, to have a SMART plan for how best to use the data to help the service, its clients and its practitioners.

A SMART approach (see Chapter 6) to a dataset this big and complex needs expert help to analyse it intelligently, but services have little or no money for this. Generally, the solution is to look for collaborators or partners. Try a local university statistics or psychology department and explain that this large, well-anonymised, dataset could be used for final-year student, master's and doctoral dissertation work, and ensure that the consent from clients and the data handling meet information governance requirements for this to happen. It can be wise to have a staff 'data liaison group' or 'research and audit group'.

Such work needs terms of reference. Start from the assumption that no therapist or service is intending to do harm and commit that analyses will not single out or name and shame therapists or sub-departments. If outcomes are found that are worse than expected, this commitment means that these can investigated constructively, but have a plan for that: such investigations should start by asking if there has been a data entry error? If not, then other questions might include the following: Are the results because of higher deprivation in a particular area? Are there any systemic difficulties (e.g. a manager on long-term sick leave) that mean that a service or practitioner is not getting the support they need? It is important too that this does not just turn the work from therapist-bashing to manager-bashing: few if any services are currently funded to provide all the support that might be optimal. The aspiration is that exploration for systematic differences in outcomes should help to improve service provision and not be persecutory.

Therapist identification: confidentiality and transparency

The idea that therapists will be compared on their OM data can create strong anxieties and raises a question about how therapists are identified in any analyses. Such anxieties should be respected, and how this is handled will impact on therapists' goodwill and engagement in the data collection and analysis. Some services may want full transparency in which everyone can see each other's identities, whereas others may want each therapist to see their own results but not be able to identify peers.

In general, we recommend that latter scenario, although it should be remembered that there are limits to this discretion and in discussions it is likely that at least some therapists will be able to work out the identity of others from the data. One example is where only two therapists work in a single location: it can make obvious sense for their data to be compared within location, but it is then impossible for their identities to be hidden. Glib promises of confidentiality will not work but a non-punitive overall approach may encourage groups of practitioners to volunteer to share their data reports. Where data-sharing groups emerge, they should be encouraged to propose questions to the service about how to understand and explore their data. Then a key question for the director is how much time to protect for such groups to think reflectively about their data. It is important to recognise that good collaboration takes time.

How to decide what to look for in your service's data?

Again, be SMART: realistic and not over-ambitious. Try to identify a small number of things that may be useful indicators of successes or failures in service delivery. Considering individual episodes of contact with the service, these might include:

- Long waits to be seen for assessment
- Long waits to start therapy
- Rates of non-attendance at the first session
- Rates of non-attendance at subsequent sessions
- Rates of opt-out earlier than had been planned/expected
- 'Outcomes' on the measures, i.e. scores on last completions during therapy.

As you can see, OM change is not the only issue and it must be considered in context.

Analyses must be in digestible chunks. It is usually sensible to have monthly reporting of selected statistics by locations. This will probably reveal systematic differences across sites. These can help the service to start asking questions about what may be behind these differences and may start to address whether the mapping of therapist time and therapies to community sites is optimal.

Focus one: opting out

It is essential to pick some key parameters and to look at them sensibly and with an open mind, asking yourself how one factor may impact on another. In this example, we look at high early opt-out from therapy as a question. It is easy to think that this must be problematic, but it can occur for a range of reasons and is not necessarily down to dissatisfaction with the service or the therapist.

Having chosen a focus, you need to choose how to explore it. We will start by looking at the relationship between the number of sessions attended and the PHQ change. As this is a stepped care service, clients are offered either six- or 24-session therapies, so we need to consider the different therapy durations offered.

Using scattergrams to explore opting-out

We have already seen a scattergram: the Jacobson plot described in Chapter 5 is an elaborated scattergram of final scores against initial scores. Figure 8.1 is a scattergram of change in PHQ score (y axis) against number of sessions attended (x axis) for a tranche of 3,187 completed client episodes from our hypothetical service.

Every client who has a starting and a final score creates a point in this plot. As we saw in Chapter 5, overprinting is an issue for scattergrams of large datasets, and it happens in Figure 8.1 when two or more clients have the same PHQ change and number of sessions attended so their points superimpose and look no different from a single client's point. This makes the visual impression of the data misleading. In Figures 5.6 and 5.7 in Chapter 5, we handled overprinting by changing client points to circles proportional to the number of clients at that point. Two different tricks have been used to handle overprinting

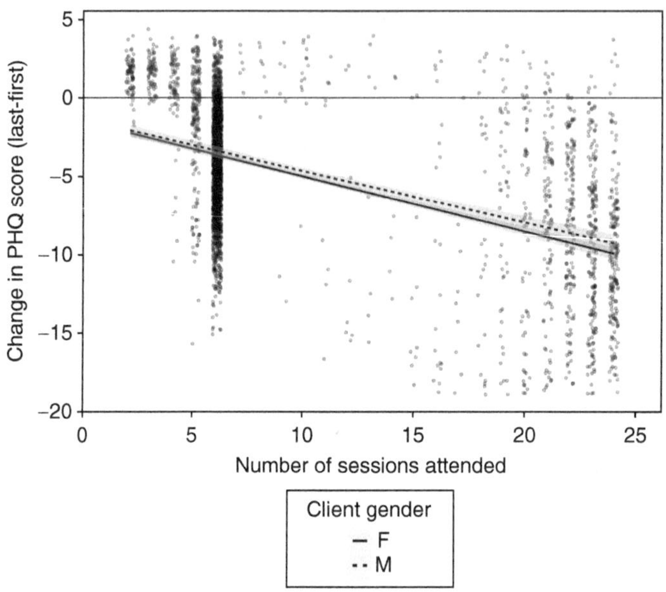

Figure 8.1 Scatterplot with linear regression: PHQ change against sessions attended

in Figure 8.1. Firstly, the points have been 'jittered', i.e. moved a little randomly to the right or left and above and below their actual number of sessions attended and score change. In addition, the points are translucent so that when they overlap, they darken, thus conveying the point density.

The horizontal reference line across the plot marks no score change from starting to finishing score: it is immediately easy to see that far more clients showed a fall in PHQ score than a rise. We can also see that there is a tendency for those who came for more sessions to show a larger drop in PHQ score. One way of making this relationship easier to see is to use a statistical procedure called linear regression. Linear regression puts the straight line that best fits the relationship between the two variables in the plot, here PHQ score change and numbers of sessions attended. In Figure 8.1, we have plotted two regression lines according to the gender of the clients, with the females marked by the solid line and the males by the dashed line. We can see there is a small difference between the lines by gender. The shaded areas around those lines mark their 95% confidence intervals (see Chapter 5). Each line lies outside the confidence interval around the other line, indicating that gender has a systematic effect. For all session counts men show less mean PHQ improvement than women and the slightly flatter slope of their line compared to that for the women shows that, generally, they show less PHQ score improvement per session.

The densely populated vertical bands of clients' points to the left of the plot show the high numbers in the step 2 work. Following these bands across from left to right, we see a relatively unpopulated area made up of clients opting out early from step 3 (24-session) work, followed by an increase in numbers opting out later in the step 3 work. The final, more dense bands of points represent those clients completing nearly all 24 sessions.

Many of those completing only one to four sessions had change well above the regression lines, showing a score deterioration. This suggests that those sloped lines representing a relationship between PHQ change and numbers of sessions attended probably do not represent well those relationships for either step 2 or step 3. What happens if we separate the two steps?

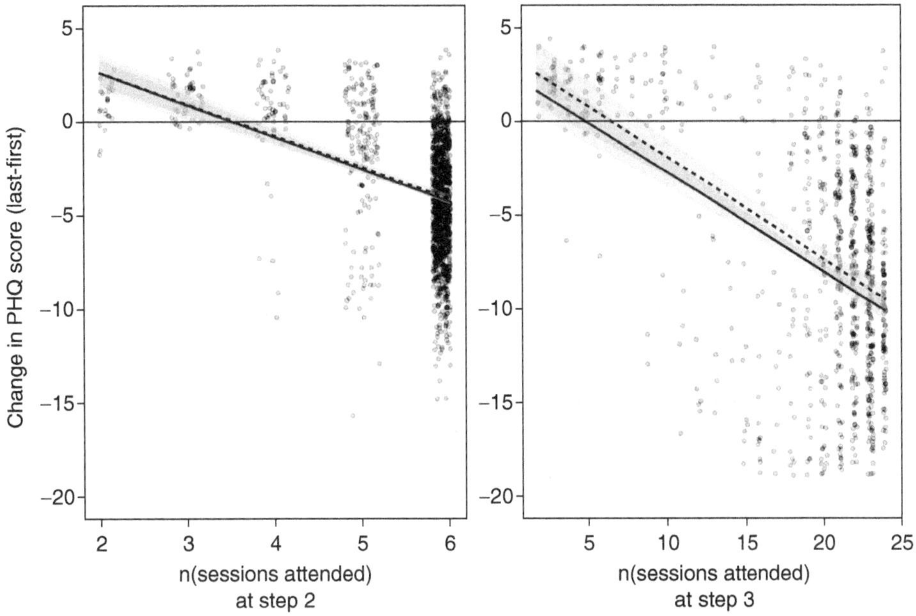

Figure 8.2 Scatterplot: PHQ change against sessions attended by care step

Figure 8.2 separates the data from the two steps, sometimes called 'facetted' plot. Now we can see that the data for the two steps are rather different. The y axes have the same scales for both steps but the x axes are different, reflecting the different numbers of sessions offered. We can see that there is almost no difference between men and women in step 2, but that in step 3 the men start and end at higher mean PHQ score changes than the women, although the slopes by gender are similar, showing that each gender, in general, gets the same improvement for more sessions attended. A finding that is probably much more useful for the service than these gender effects is that we can see that many of those opting out before the planned numbers of sessions showed deteriorations in PHQ score, i.e. above the 'no change' reference line.

Looking at these data prompts a review in the service, and it is suggested that some clients being mapped to step 2, perhaps particularly those opting out early with score deteriorations, might benefit more from step 3. It is known that therapists in step 2 are less experienced than those in step 3 and it is felt likely that there will be improvement in step 2 outcomes if more of the clients felt to be more challenging for inexperienced therapists could be mapped to step 3. However, it is recognised that this could not be done without increasing waiting times.

Turning to the step 3 data in the right hand panel of Figure 8.2, a tabulation of this data would show that 81.1% of the clients (751) are opting out before 24 sessions. Of these, some are showing PHQ score deterioration whereas most are showing PHQ score improvements, some of which are very large. It was already known that many clients opt out in step 3 and that, even with quite rapid discharge after non-attendance, this wastes sessions. With this in mind, the service can look more closely at changes in PHQ-9 scores in relation to opting out. The use of graphics is invaluable here and we will use the plots we introduced in Chapter 5 to explore distributions and relationships. We will also use confidence intervals to keep in focus whether apparent relationships are likely to prove robust and recur, or where they are likely to be down to sampling vagaries.

We are interested in PHQ-9 change in relation to opting out. A sensible first way to see if early opting-out relates to improvement is to use notched boxplots. Figure 8.3, a facetted boxplot, shows change on the PHQ from the first to last scores against opting-out. The two facets are for the two levels in the stepped care which dictate the maximum number of sessions offered: six for 'Step 2' and 24 for 'Step 3'. The steps are shown in the headers of the facets.

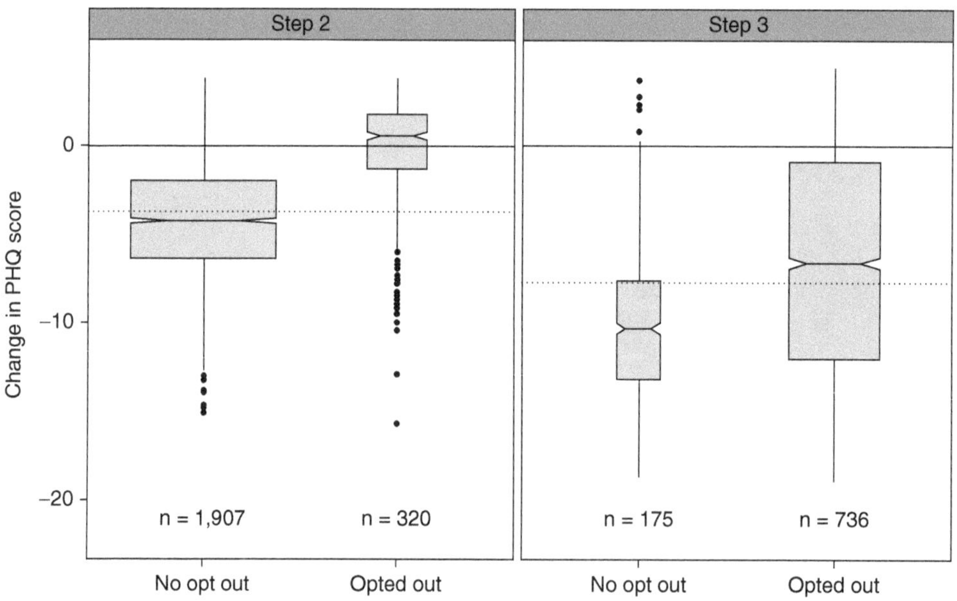

Figure 8.3 Notched boxplots of PHQ change by care step and opting-out

As before, the solid horizontal line marks no change and the dotted horizontal lines mark the median change within the stepped care level. Here are some key things to note:

1. The plots confirm that opting-out is associated with less improvement within both levels.
2. It can be seen that over half of the 320 opting out of step 2 actually had a deterioration in PHQ score (as the median, i.e. the waist of the box, is above the no change line).
3. The notches on the boxes, showing the confidence intervals around the median changes, are tightly pinched around the median so we can safely conclude that the differences are not just sampling vagaries.
4. We can also see that the median fall in PHQ score in the step 3 interventions is greater than in the step 2 interventions and that the median fall in PHQ even of those opting out of step 3 interventions is greater than for those completing step 2 interventions.

Knowing there was a systematic link between opting-out and change in PHQ score, the service also wanted to know how many sessions clients who opt out early actually attended, which is shown in Figure 8.4. From the downward whisker for step 2, we can see that everyone attended at least two sessions, but that was necessary in order to have measured PHQ change from the first session so the graph must omit those opting out after just one session. For step 3, we can see that very few attended only two sessions. These are shown as dots as they are rare enough to be defined as 'outliers' in the conventions of boxplots.

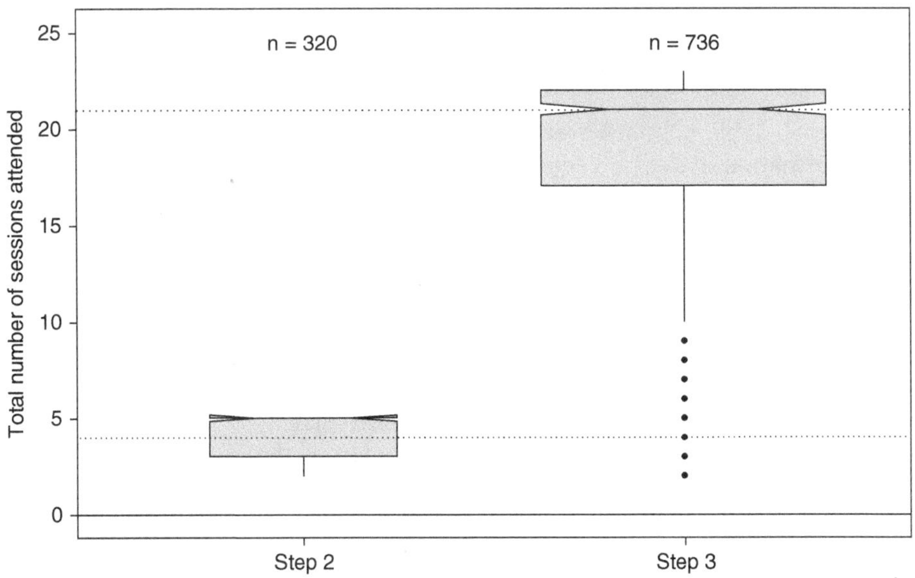

Figure 8.4 Notched boxplots of sessions attended by those opting out, by care step

Looking at the upper limits we know that those opting out of step 2 could not have attended six sessions and we see that the upper limit was five sessions, as we would expect. We can see that the median attendance (the dotted line) of the step 2 opt-out group was four sessions. In fact, this boxplot is a good example of instances where the numbers are such that a table is more informative: Table 8.1 shows the numbers of sessions attended by those opting out of step 2. Clearly, this table tells us everything about attendance by those opting out in this group, just as Table 8.2 tells us all about the opting-out in both groups.

Table 8.1 Breakdown of sessions attended for step 2 non-completers

Sessions attended	**n**
1	34
2	57
3	45
4	57
5	161

Table 8.2 Breakdown of sessions attended for non-completers

	1	**2**	**3**	**4**	**5**	**6**	**7**	**8**	**9**	**10**	**11**	**12**	**13**	**14**	**15**	**16**	**17**	**18**	**19**	**20**	**21**	**22**	**23**
Step 2	34	57	45	57	161																		
Step 3	15	16	22	14	13	18	6	7	7	14	9	8	9	6	10	21	9	26	46	59	107	135	174

Although Table 8.2 does break down the counts of early opt-out and has all that information, it is also becoming rather indigestible. However, the boxplot in Figure 8.4, even though it loses information compared to the tabulation, does makes it easier to get a sense of the distributions of early opt-out. This is a very typical issue when trying to understand therapy service data: different presentations have different strengths.

At this point, the service is gaining some understanding of opting-out and PHQ change but would really like to see if they can improve things. Closer examination of the statistics underlying the scattergrams of PHQ change against sessions attended (Figures 8.1 and 8.2) would show that there was an interesting variation of change in the step 3 opting-out group as the standard deviation of change for them was 6.5 versus 4.5 for those not opting out (remember that SD is a measure of the scatter around the mean).

From the bottom edge of the PHQ change boxes in Figure 8.3, i.e. the lower quartiles, we can see that 25% of those opting out had a PHQ improvement that was not much worse than for those completing the 24 sessions. It is impossible to see the exact difference in the boxplot, but it is a change of -12 for those opting out and -13.2 is achieved by 25% of those who completed all 24 sessions offered. In other words, about a quarter who are opting out within step 3 appear to do as well in terms of PHQ change as the bottom quarter of those continuing for all 24 sessions. This suggests that it may be worth looking more closely at the trajectories of change in those who opt out but appear to have done well in terms of PHQ change.

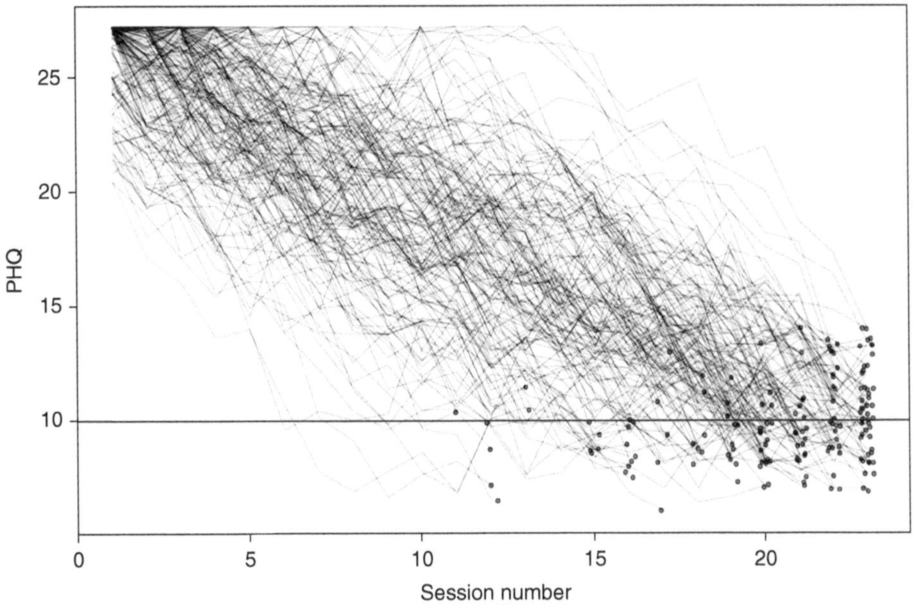

Figure 8.5 Stretched cat's cradle plot showing early opt-out PHQ trajectories

Figure 8.5 shows the trajectories of PHQ change for the 159 clients who opted out of step 3 but who had a PHQ improvement of at least 13. The final scores for each client are marked with a point. The horizontal reference line is the cutting point for 'clinical significance' of score. Again, these have been 'jittered' horizontally a little so that clients ending on the same score at the same session do not overprint each other. We can see that these clients started with high PHQ scores from 20.3 to 27 (the maximum possible). That they had high starting scores is to some extent a corollary of our selecting them for achieving PHQ score drops of at least 13: you have to start above 13 to achieve that! The service tabulated the numbers of sessions these clients had attended (Table 8.3).

Table 8.3 Breakdown of sessions attended by 'success' opt-outs

Number of sessions	11	12	13	15	16	17	18	19	20	21	22	23
n	1	4	2	5	9	5	7	11	19	22	27	47

These are not data from a real service, but if they were, the service might want to explore why so many clients opt out in the later sessions. Is there some difficulty with managing endings or saying goodbye? Given that some clients in this opting-out group have quite a dramatic improvement, the robustness of this could be checked by looking at whether they return to the service more rapidly than other clients. Non-return might suggest that early termination is associated with sustained change, whereas a high return or re-referral might suggest that a flight into health had not allowed for the gains in therapy to be embedded or consolidated. The answers to these questions could have implications as to how best to manage endings and the best way of using the large number of sessions 'released' by early opt-out (the 159 early opt-outs with good PHQ improvement would have released a theoretical total of 575 sessions).

Focus two: are social deprivation and therapist experience related to PHQ change?

This last exploration had raised questions about the mapping of clients to steps and about the training and post-training experience of therapists in the service. The therapists agreed that there were very marked differences in training and experience between them, but also argued that some of the service centres were in areas of high social deprivation and others in areas of very low deprivation. It seemed wise to look at whether these factors related to PHQ change and, if so, whether more thought might be given to mapping therapists to centres considering therapy experience and local deprivation. We are going to use another method of illustrating data to address whether these factors related to PHQ change: the forest plot.

Using forest plots to explore PHQ change by social deprivation and therapist experience

Like the grouped boxplot, the forest plot is good for exploring differences between groups and it can be thought of as just the belt and notch of the boxplot, i.e. a plot of central location with its confidence interval. Forest plots have become very widely used in systematic reviews of published data and they can, in principle, be used for any statistic that can have a confidence interval. Figure 8.6 is a very simple forest plot which the service could use to see if the change in the PHQ scores relates to area deprivation, measured here as a five-level classification of the socio-demographic challenges in the area around each centre.

The five-level socio-demographic challenge classification was based on health service data deprivation indices for each centre in which the therapists are based. The five are ordered from least deprivation, level 1, to most deprivation at level 5. In this forest plot, the central location used is the mean, shown by the central square points for each deprivation level and the 95%

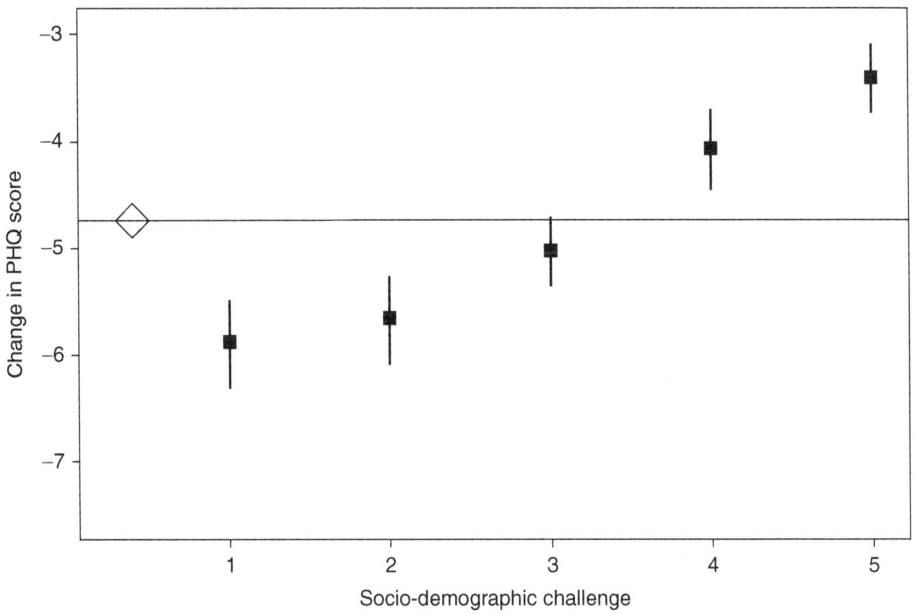

Figure 8.6 Forest plot of PHQ change against local deprivation index

confidence interval is shown by the vertical bars through those points. In addition, the forest plot has a reference line which is the overall mean and the diamond on the left, around that line, is the 95% confidence interval around that overall mean. That is much tighter than the CI for each group as the number of clients contributing to that CI is about five times larger than the number for each group (remember, generally the larger the sample, the smaller the confidence interval).

We can see in Figure 8.6 that there is a clear relationship between deprivation and the mean drop in PHQ scores, with less difference between deprivation levels 1 and 2 than between the remaining deprivation levels. This finding enabled the service to identify those centres which posed greater demographic challenges and to start discussions with the commissioners and the centres around possible options to address this, such as increasing the number of sessions allowed in the group 4 and 5 deprivation centres.

The therapists agreed there was no simple categorisation of levels of training and experience, but a system based on factual data from all the therapists was collectively agreed at a service away-day. The levels were defined partly so they would split all the therapists into five roughly equal-sized groups. Figure 8.7 is a forest plot showing mean PHQ change against therapist experience facetted by step. The findings were dramatically clear, with the mean improvement for most training and experience levels (represented in the forest plot by the squares) clearly different and the differences between the means generally bigger than the CIs (the vertical bars).

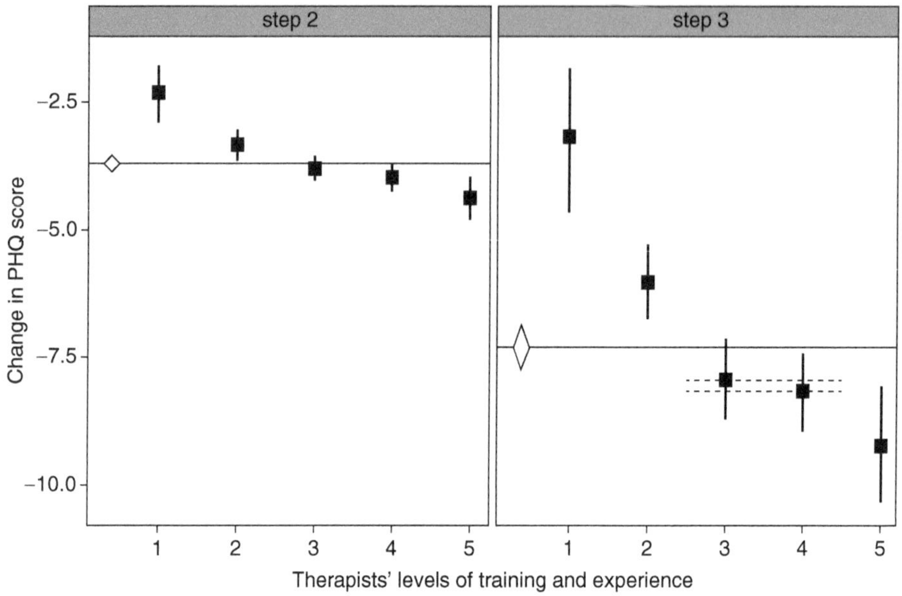

Figure 8.7 Forest plot of PHQ change against therapist experience/training and care step

Within each step, PHQ improvement is related to greater training and experience with the smallest difference between levels 3 and 4. Far more clients are being seen in step 2, hence the confidence intervals around the means are tighter there. Within step 3, the relatively small number of therapists with only level 1 training and experience is shown in the wide CI (vertical bar length) for this group, and there are clear differences in mean PHQ improvement between them and all four other levels as well as between level 2 and levels 3 and 4 and between level 5 and all the other levels. However, the difference between levels 3 and 4 could well be down to sampling vagaries given that the mean change for each level is within the CI for the other level. (To help you see this we have drawn dashed lines through the means for each of these two groups and made them long enough to show clearly how the mean for each group lies within the CI of the mean for the other group).

Researcher's equipoise – how not to mis-interpret data

One of the big anxieties for therapists is that differences in their outcome scores might be used to create a league table of 'good' and 'poor' therapists. There are some proponents of this approach who advocate use of such tables to remove therapists with poor change results. Of course, differences in outcome scores may indeed reflect the abilities of the therapists – in which case managerial and supervisory exploration, probably ideally starting with support, is indicated. However, it is important to be careful about what might cause these findings: to have 'equipoise' about possible causes not to jump to any particular one. Differences in change scores may be due to a whole range of factors, for example:

1. Are there consistent differences in terms of the client group assigned to particular therapists? Such factors might include: social deprivation, employment, diagnosis, English as an additional language, etc.
2. Are there consistent differences between referrers? Are referrals appropriate to the service offered? Perhaps outcomes are affected by the subtle support or undermining of psychological therapies by other practitioners in the health centre.
3. Are there differences in the experience of the practitioners available, or the supervision, ongoing learning opportunities and support available to practitioners in different services? One service might have therapists who work alone or who are very isolated; another might have therapists who have all been practising for over 20 years; and a third service might have lots of honorary trainee therapists, but also journal clubs, reflective practice support, etc.

A good statistician can help you to unpick those differences on measured variables. There are many ways to look at these issues, and although it is still relatively early days for this in psychotherapy and counselling, it is also important to remember that no methods are robust when numbers of particular subgroups are very small.

It is clear that assessing differences in outcomes without statistical advice and without careful conversations with the therapists, supervisors and managers can risk making ill-informed and bad decisions based on the data. It is also crucial to remember that no statistician or statistical method can tell you anything about unmeasured factors: only the service as a whole can try to take into account issues like referrer attitudes, quality of the working environment, etc.

Comparing data with that from other services and with published data

All the points made in Chapter 7 apply equally for services as for individual practitioners. While the political issues are different from those for individual practitioners, the statistical issues are the same. Here again, it will be worthwhile for services to compare their own data with published data. As with individual practitioners, pooling of data from several services within networks will enable the exploration of rare issues that would not be possible even from the data of a single large service. Examples of such events might include therapies conducted using interpreters, the impact of ethnic difference in client–therapist dyads, etc.

Summary

In some ways, promoting service evaluation reveals a kind of paradox in the work of routine outcome monitoring: on the one hand, it can be simple and valuable, and on the other hand, it is complex and can be misleading if handled badly. Try not to be put off by this and remember that having ROM data adds to what we had before.

Of course, it is valuable to know if clients are reporting scores that suggest improvement or deterioration over the course of therapy. However, therapy is complex and the more complex your system becomes (delays in starting therapy, different models and durations of therapy, different types of client, different demographics, different therapists), the more circumspect one must be when making assumptions about causes and correlations.

Make sure that your mechanisms for data collection are easily complied with and are reliable. Ensure that you have simple but robust systems for collecting, recording and storing data. When it comes to analysing and interpreting your results, safeguard your and your clients' work by encouraging ways of connecting in groups to explore, interrogate, investigate and talk about your findings.

9

Working with clients and supervisors when using outcome measures

In Chapters 7 and 8 we have looked at how to plan data collection and analysis for both individual practitioners and for a large service. This chapter turns to communication about measures and change data. We stress that you can only communicate effectively if you understand the 'why?', 'what?', 'where?' and 'when?' of your data collection. The 'why?' is crucial and develops some of the themes in the last two chapters about knowing what you are trying to achieve with data. The 'what?', 'where?' and 'when?' link back to Chapter 6 and a SMART approach to ensuring that your data collection fits your work situation. We now look at these questions in more detail and then use them to look at how you communicate about measures with clients and with supervisors/supervisees. However, running through the chapter is the reality that even in single-handed practice, therapy and therapy data collection also involve external stakeholders - managers, commissioners, insurance funding and registration bodies - and holding these audiences in mind is essential for effective work.

Why? – embedded or external measures

The first 'why?' question is this key distinction first introduced in Chapter 1.

1. Are you aiming to look at data collected outside the therapy room, and typically collated after treatments finish, e.g. as part of quality assurance, service improvement, audit or formal outcome research? Is your 'why' to inform others?
2. Or are your data being used and discussed within sessions, to shape the therapy?

If OM data are considered during therapy, particularly within sessions, this changes the therapy and probably affects the client's use of the OM. You cannot 'unknow' what you have seen in answers or scores and this will affect how you and the client work in the room together: measuring in this way becomes a part of the therapy. It is highly likely that a focus on the OM in the session will change how clients experience and respond to the OM next time. If we compare OM scores from therapies where measures are not seen by the therapist with ones where they are, we are not comparing like with like, even if the actual measure used is the same one.

This is not an argument for or against embedding measures in therapy, but it is against asking one OM to do two jobs at once. If we want OMs to guide therapy *and* we want to use them to compare our work with others' work, we should use two different measures, one for each task. Both measures and purposes need to be explained, which makes for a slightly more complicated discussion than when just using one approach, but that is not a huge challenge. We distinguish two different uses of embedded OMs. A reminder of our terminology is set out in Box 9.1.

Box 9.1 Key terms

EM – Embedded Measures/Measurement
Looking at measures *within* the therapy, as part of the therapy. EM inevitably changes the relationship the client and therapist have with the measures.

ECM – Embedded Change Measurement
As with EM, OMs are completed *within* the therapy, but in ECM the scores may be used to steer the therapy, often designating change as 'on track' or 'off track'.

External measures
OMs not used within sessions.

Embedded measures are not new!

Although EM and ECM have grown markedly in the last decade or so, it is important to remember that quite disparate modalities have used forms of sessional ratings for decades. This is probably most often associated with Behavioural and CBT approaches in the form of clients' ratings such as:

'On a scale of one to ten how difficult was it to get out of the house this week?' Of course, it is not unusual for therapists working in other modalities to start sessions by asking: *'How has the last week been for you on a scale of...'*. Solution-focused therapies (SFT) also have ratings, and as we have noted before, SFT therapists, in line with the mantra 'problem talk is problem talk', will *not* want ratings of problems but of positives and solutions. We call these EM.

What *is* new is using the same measures for all clients and then comparing change in any one therapy against data from large referential datasets of scores from other therapies. What we call ECM is the use of such referential data to generate 'on track/off track' feedback to the therapist or to both therapist and client. In this scenario, 'on track' refers to the OM scores comparing favourably with the external dataset and 'off track' when results on the OMs used are poorer that the referential dataset. This can give potentially useful information, but we have concerns that the enthusiasm for this may overvalue the idea and ignore its problems.

Model specificity

The 'why?' of data collection should be congruent with the 'why?' of therapy: the rationale of the modality being used, and indeed of any individual therapist's way of working. As we noted before, some modalities have seen overt change ratings as antithetical to the principles of their therapy. Clearly, these therapists are not uninterested in change: we believe that all therapists have internal ratings of how the client is doing and look out for indicators that things are getting better or worse. The issue is about the particular use of overt and standardised measures within the therapy.

In the psychodynamic modality, many practitioners feel that bringing measures into the session is at odds with the close attention, by therapist and client, to what the client brings to the session unconsciously. On this argument, placing OM completion into the session, particularly at the start, will anchor things in conscious evaluation, deflect the client from speaking about whatever comes to mind and change the transference relationship. We believe that this logic is sound and a reason why EM is not appropriate for all therapies, but it should not prevent ROM where the measures lie outside the therapy.

To give a simple example: within a psychodynamic framework it can be entirely 'on track' for a person to feel worse, sometimes much worse, before things make a turn for the better. Clients are encouraged to explore the roots of their distress and this may lead them to remember and reflect on painful relationships or past traumas. Recognising this, and accepting that this apparent worsening in how someone feels is possibly to be expected and may be reflected in self-report measure scores, is something psychodynamic therapists and supervisors need to consider. Another example, understandable in most therapy models, is that there can be strong evidence of positive changes in the client's external life and/or their use of the therapy, yet this may go with some marked deterioration in self-report questionnaire scores. Typically, this might happen because the client is starting to see him/herself differently: a *response shift* in psychometric jargon. For example, a client may have avoided acknowledging specific difficulties, for example in their relationships, but as they start to change there may be relief or a feeling of potential change for the person, their family and friends which might go hand in hand with a more realistic appraisal of their difficulties appearing as a deterioration in scores on particular measures.

The issues are not specific to psychodynamic thinking. In some systemic therapies, and some humanistic-integrative therapies, incongruent trajectories might be expected as someone moves from a 'failed solution' or from a state that has lacked resilience and authenticity, but which has been comfortable and familiar for perhaps many years, to one that is new, currently scary, but which may in the longer term be more adaptive and better for the client. It behoves supervisor and therapist to think carefully about these ways of understanding the client's scores and to explore whether the client may be saying something important through the measure which they may feel unable to say, or of which they are unaware, in the sessions.

Notwithstanding the logic, incongruence between score change and the experience in the sessions should never just be accepted as 'expected' as 'things get worse before they get better' or other similar arguments. Nor should it be simply assumed that one or both of the measure or quality of the therapy is awry. The discrepancy needs to be thought about carefully. For example, in psychodynamic therapies, discrepant trajectories should really only appear when some change is taking place that is undoing a previous defensive state or shifting an unconscious conflict.

As well as congruence with the way the therapist works, ECM needs to fit the client and we have yet to see acknowledgement that some clients may simply not be able to use the OM whose referential data shapes an ECM model. As we have explored in several chapters already, no OM generalises to all clients. We worry that therapists trained in the ECM model may work well, and perhaps cheaply, with literate clients with mild problems but be at a loss with other and perhaps more challenging clients.

We have gone into some detail about why imposing ECM on all therapies may be misguided because we believe that an over-simplified understanding of ECM risks damaging a more general adoption of *appropriate* ROM and that it undermines the thinking about 'why?'. We would like to believe that these strategic and design issues are discussed during training and in services imposing a particular OM, but we are not convinced that this happens routinely. Sadly, when a therapist whose training did not cover these things at all is forced by management or politicians to use measures that feel alien to their way of working, it sets people up to be resistant to OMs generally. Open-minded interest in this area of work will help us to discover which OMs are suitable for which models and clients, and genuinely improve our understanding of their benefits and limitations.

If we have thought through the 'why?' of using ROMs in our setting, we can move to 'what?', 'where?', 'when?' and towards actual conversations with clients.

What? Where? and When?

Whether you work as an individual practitioner or in a larger service you will already have routines in place. These routines shape how you arrange an initial meeting, how clients can contact you between sessions, how you discuss the contract of your work, how you manage breaks for holidays or illness, how you invoice for the work done, and so on. OM data collection must fit your routines if you are to gain useful information. Just as you cannot communicate about measures if you are not clear about the 'why?' of using them, you will not communicate persuasively if you are not also clear about the 'what?', 'where?' and 'when?'. Ignoring these questions means that OMs will get overlooked or completed casually or even provocatively, and data completeness and quality will deteriorate perhaps to the point when analyses will be misleading.

Understanding 'what?', 'where?' and 'when?' should be shared with everyone in contact with clients and the details will vary between services and practices. In managed services, as we noted in Chapter 8, it is common for therapists to resent data collection, feeling that it is imposed 'from above' and they will neglect the 'what?', 'where?' and 'when?'. At other times, therapists simply feel unfamiliar with quantitative data and its analyses, and anxieties will interfere with collecting it. These issues can be mitigated if time is taken to discuss data collection with everybody, and we hope this book helps therapists to feel more familiar with OM data and its processes. However, if issues are not discussed and concerns allayed, therapists' anxieties will be communicated, deliberately or unintentionally, to clients, with potential impacts on the data.

ECM and EM practicalities

The more OMs are embedded into therapies, the more the 'what?', 'where?' and 'when?' will need to be explained, and those discussions are located within the therapies. If you are working in an ECM or EM framework, it helps to think about practicalities and the discussions that may be needed. If the measures are completed on paper, do you watch closely over the client's shoulder? Do you take the questionnaires when they finish and go through them then, and perhaps pick up on particular items, as well as computing the scores (if that is easy to do)? If the client inputs data directly into software using a tablet or keyboard, how does that happen? Can both you and the client see the screen and the data?

If you are using software, what information is visible to you inside and outside the session? Does the system give you a matrix of the item scores over time, perhaps colouring them to indicate change? Some systems use 'traffic lights': green for 'on track' improvement and red for deterioration or 'off track' slow improvement. Whatever the system does, think about the following:

- Does the system you are using generate subscale scores as well as an overall score? Do they add value or over-complicate things?
- Does it give you a plot of change of the accumulating pattern of scores over time?

- If so, is that plot coloured to indicate some referential values for scores, perhaps above or below a clinical/non-clinical cutting point?
- Is it divided into quartiles or centiles (Chapter 5)?
- Does it give measurement error bars and/or confidence intervals (Chapter 5)?
- Does it have 'on track/off track' traffic lights?
- If the results are given directly to the client, how might they react to this? Will it leave the client feeling slotted into technology or will they feel that they have been given reassuringly detailed attention?
- Are there clients or client groups who may have specific or particular reactions? Will some feel that the scores are a comment on their performance and feel a failure if their symptoms are worsening? What might be the impact on a client who is socially anxious? Is there a risk they might skew their scores to comply with what they perceive as therapist expectations that they should be getting better? For other clients, this kind of external feedback may be reassuring.
- How will you pick up and respond to these reactions in the session?

Focusing on specific items in EM

It is important that therapists are familiar with the measures they are using and know whether they want to focus on individual items or not. Some measures have a 'risk' score which therapists are alerted to in EM. For obvious reasons, many therapists will focus on these risk items and, while there is a logic to this, it can convey to the client that the therapist is only interested in risk. Some therapists might think they should target and focus on the highest scored items, but this can be misleading. For good psychometric reasons, many measures have items that are tuned high, e.g. *'I have made plans to kill myself'*, but other items that are tuned low, e.g. *'I have been irritable when with other people'*. This means that the item on which the person gives the highest score may not reflect their most severe problems.

One focusing strategy is to ask the client if any item was particularly important for them. As therapy proceeds, for some clients it may be helpful to focus on items that are changing in a positive direction. This technique is called TRIM (Tracking the Response to Items in Measures) and by focusing on positive changes on specific items it can embed a solution-focused stance even within largely problem-oriented measures. It may be particularly useful for clients who have had psychotic problems or have been deeply entrenched in their problems for a very long time.

The generic guide is that what you do in your own practice should be congruent with your clinical theory, be flexible to attend to the impact on the individual client and have a good fit with any consultation or supervision you have in relation to your work, which brings us to our next section.

Mixing idiographic and nomothetic measures

Idiographic and client-generated measures (Chapters 2 and 4) allow any client to create their own questionnaire. Think how to explain these measures; for example, if you choose to use the client-generated measures during the session but a nomothetic one outside the session for a kind of audit. You may want to say something like this:

As you'll see, as well as the measures we generate together about your particular hopes for change, I also use another measure at the start of therapy and then one once a month which has fixed items and which we will not discuss as part of our work. I do that so I am able to compare my work with other therapists.

This brings us to conversations with clients. We will give some specific examples below which we hope will help you to think what is best for your own situation.

Talking about the measures with clients

If you are collecting data for your own interest and monitoring, you should have found it fairly easy to sort out your 'why?', 'what?', 'where?' and 'when?' questions without having much external stakeholder influence.

Why are you doing it? ***What*** are you collecting: which measure or measures? ***Where*** will you give the measures? In the waiting room? By post? With your invoice? Linked with this, ***when*** will you give the measures? Before every session? After every session? Weekly? Monthly? Just pre- and post-therapy? Will you send follow-up measures after you have finished therapy? As we set out earlier, your choice of EM, ROM or both will lead to different decisions and different conversations. We gave some examples of how someone might go about this in Chapter 7.

If the data collection was required by commissioners or managers, it is wise to ask them for explanations. In principle, explanations should come from those requiring the data. Sometimes when data is required by commissioners or managers, it may feel incongruent with what you do in the sessions. If so, find a form of words that handles this honestly without undermining the data collection process or conveying insecurity. An example that could be used in an EM service might go something like this:

We are required to collect these data. In fact, whether we do or do not makes a difference to the funding of the service and is part of the service audit and quality improvement. Of course, what we will talk about in the sessions will give a much richer and more complete picture of your life and your struggles than the measures do. However, these measures provide another way, a kind of simple summary, looking at whether what we offer is helpful. NHS commissioners and managers want some insight into how people get on in therapy here. What I find works is for you and I to go through these questionnaires rapidly at the start of each session. Sometimes it will be that your responses to some of the items point to things we might want to talk about, at other times you will have things you already know you want to talk about and we can go straight to that. Very occasionally, I might come back to an item as I may feel it was important and might be telling us something we are missing.

That is probably an example that would cover working as a humanistic, psychodynamic or couple counsellor in many services. We think it conveys a confidence in the practitioner's own ways of working and that the client should aim to communicate with the practitioner directly rather than through the measures. However, it avoids denigrating the measures or the logic behind them. It is worth anticipating and thinking through a few follow-up questions clients might have and how you would want to answer them. Examples might include:

- 'What if I want to have my own data so I can think about it?'
- 'What if I don't want to fill these in at all?'
- 'What if I would like us to discuss something from the questionnaire?'
- 'What if I don't like one item or want to change it or miss it out?'

It may be wise to find out an officially approved answer to some such questions, but we think it is perfectly appropriate to say 'I'm really sorry, I don't know, but I can ask', or 'that's interesting, I haven't been asked that before. I will pass the question on and someone from the department will contact you who *can* answer that for the service.'

OM data in supervision and consultation

Communicating about OMs with clients is probably considered by almost all therapists using OMs. However, we are less confident that as much thought goes into talking about OM data in supervision and consultation. As ever, the hope is that supervisors and supervisees can find ways to use OM data that are comfortable and congruent with their own and the service expectations. The simple criterion is that the OMs, and scores, can be spoken about openly and thoughtfully in supervision.

It can be important to distinguish between 'line management (supervision)' and 'clinical supervision/consultation' as their tasks and aims do differ and may need different use of OM data.

Line management

In some services it is possible to compare therapists' change data and this may be seen as a central part of line management. We do not recommend glib comparison of therapists' change data where there is any non-random allocation of clients to therapists. It is easy to overlook how differences in referral processes and the different complexities of clients (social deprivation being just one important indicator here) may mean that different therapists have very different outcomes.

Having said that, we would encourage services to review with therapists a designated proportion of 'best' and 'worst' outcomes where sufficient numbers of clients are seen. This is an appropriate component of sensible service audit and quality improvement. Similarly, we would encourage an intermittent, non-persecutory review of aggregated change data at intervals, providing there are sufficient data to be informative.

Clinical supervision

Where therapies involve EM or ECM, the data must be accessible in supervision and the supervisor and supervisee(s) will decide together how much to focus on the data and how much to focus on other aspects of the therapy work. One challenge, probably mainly outside CBT, is that trainees and younger therapists may be more familiar with, and more comfortable with, change measures than older supervisors and consultants, and this may need to be acknowledged to avoid supervision and OM data pulling in opposing directions. Another related challenge, again sometimes connected to differences in age and experience, arises where a supervisor/consultant is external to the therapist's service and does not like the OM usage expected in the service. This can create difficult triangulation issues around measures and can become unhelpful for all concerned. The best option in such situations is to try to draw very clear boundaries so that the measures can be securely located within one side of the triangle and explicitly left out of discussions on the other.

Assuming that an interested reflective space can be found in the supervision for EM data, there are some clear scenarios that can arise. The most obvious challenge is when scores on the measures show something completely incongruent with the picture that is coming across from the narrative reporting of the session. Clearly, this requires exploration: why might a client be showing scores that, at face value, seem more troubled, or more settled, than the client's narrative and self-presentation in the sessions would suggest? Discussion with some equipoise about the values of the different data sources should help identify the possible reasons for these disparities. For example, the client may fear that their therapy will end if they appear to be better on the measure. On the other hand, they may fear that a student will get into trouble if they are not showing improvements. Discussing these possibilities in supervision helps the therapist to explore this with the client. When working in a modality and practice that ultimately trusts the conscious capabilities of both client and therapist to talk about things and find ways around collisions, ruptures and impasses, then there is nothing in EM that should undermine the therapy or the supervision. This brings us to our final point in this chapter.

Conflict of interest: measures versus therapy

This may seem like a provocative heading, but we think this arises both in communication with clients and in supervisions. This almost always happens when the necessary thinking and conversations around 'why?', 'what?', 'where?' and 'when?' have not happened.

The collision can arise when the aims for the OM data of researchers or managers, and of therapists, are not aligned. We have come across situations where supervisees feel that collecting the OM data is crucial and see missing data as a failure. For example, a client does not complete the item: *'sometimes I feel my life is not worth living'*. For an anxious trainee, who has been told that missing items compromise datasets, the need to ensure that there are no missing item scores might interfere with their clinical judgement and prevent them exploring with the client why this question is so powerful for them at this time. In this situation, responding with 'It seems like that question is leaving you with some important feelings. I wonder if we can talk about that?' is a much more appropriate response than 'That's a really important item, see if you can give some response and we can talk about it afterwards'.

Figure 9.1 Rating scale (Chapman, 2021; http://lightbulbcartoon.com/)

Reproduced by kind permission of Richard Chapman

Another example is where the client and therapist might lean too much on the OM to the extent that they can avoid talking about difficult subjects or areas. These areas will often be idiosyncratic or guilt- or shame-laden ones that do not lend themselves to easy incorporation in nomothetic measures. In a somewhat extreme scenario, the client and therapist can unwittingly collude to make everything look fine, and OM scores will come down, while the therapy fails to address what is most problematical for the client. This is more likely for understandably anxious trainee therapists and perhaps particularly with ambivalent clients, or clients with particularly complex and challenging problems. We finish on this note and hope that these issues can be increasingly discussed, locally in supervision/consultation, and generally across our fields.

Summary

In this chapter we have looked at a number of issues: particularly, what to consider when reflecting on the impact of using outcome measures in different therapeutic approaches as well as in supervision. We underlined the importance of not having a 'one size fits all' approach to this, and to considering how things can be understood differently depending on your theoretical model or framework. We have addressed in some detail the different expectations that arise when employing ECM or EM.

What is common to all of this, and necessary for constructive relationships with both clients and supervisors, is a reflective attitude. It is important to hold a mirror up to the process and think about why you are doing what you are doing and how it impacts both on the therapy and on the nature of the data you are collecting. If we get these 'why?', 'what?', 'where?' and 'when?' questions right, then ROM really can help therapy. Fail to think them through and it will actively hinder good therapy.

PART IV

COMMUNICATION AND CRITIQUE

10

A 'snapshot' review: constructive critique as a core practitioner skill

We hope that this book has given you an accessible and thorough overview of using outcome and change measures. We have covered the foundations of psychometrics and commonly used statistical procedures as well as discussing how measures can be applied in practice. Throughout we have focused on the importance of dialogue with people in the field when using outcome measurement (OM), whether they are clients or commissioners, colleagues or supervisors, researchers or clinicians. This final chapter develops this theme and is about how our data are most constructively woven into these discourses. Unless OM data contribute in a balanced way to these discussions their value is lost.

A key issue in these conversations is a capacity for constructive critique, so in this final chapter we will offer advice to help make the emerging network of evidence coherent, relevant and useful to all parties. We will do this in three sections. In the first, we look at the some of the dominant myths around therapy OMs. In the second, we list six easy-to-remember general principles and questions that we think support constructive criticism. In the third, we provide guidelines addressing some specific issues about the use of OMs.

Section 1: Dominant myths

Myth 1: 'we know what works for whom and just need to hone this'

Ironically, this argument comes from two radically different directions, the opponents of OM and the supporters of OM. The first are groups or individuals who are confident that their own model of therapy works and do not believe they need OM data to support this. The second group are those who believe that a very particular use of OMs has found the answers to questions of effectiveness and that the debate is closed. Let us take these in order.

Myth 1(a): the 'we know, we don't need OMs' argument

This has been argued by many schools of therapy. It privileges the clinician's view from the consulting room over everything else. It is understandable: a thoughtful confidence to observe what happens within the therapy room is absolutely essential for good therapy. However, this is clinically necessary but not sufficient. As we acknowledged throughout the book, OMs do not fit equally easily with all therapy modalities. Furthermore, the realm of numbers, tables, graphs and statistics is not the traditional comfort zone of most therapists. However, 'we don't need change measures' is naïve and ignores important reality checks.

As therapists, we want to believe the work we do is helpful, but this means we sometimes ignore data that are not embedded in the minute-by-minute meeting with the client: avoiding supervision or consultation is well known, but avoiding OMs is similar. Historically, professional titles conferred authority to say what was right, but this has changed through the 20th century. At the same time, therapies have been increasingly funded by public sector or third-party payers who want more than reassurance from the professionals they are paying, particularly if those messages can sound somewhat arrogant or unquestioning. This does not mean that OM data can replace theory and narrative case studies; they cannot. Nor should we overplay the importance of OM data drawn from the end of therapies. That is important but it is only one part of what we really want, which is long-term follow-up change data with an organisationally self-critical exploration of what the data tell us.

Myth 1(b): the 'we know, we don't need ROM' argument

This version of the 'we know' argument is epitomised in the NICE Guidelines (NICE, 2021, https://www.nice.org.uk/guidance) and the American Psychological Association (APA) lists of 'Empirically Supported Treatments' (EST) (APA, 2021). Unfortunately, these documents largely ignore the fact that lack of evidence *for* something is not evidence *against* it, and that many modalities and therapies omitted from these lists simply have no research evaluations, or no evaluations using methods accepted by NICE or the APA. Evaluations do require OM data, and collection of OM data varies dramatically across modalities, across client groups and across therapy formats and practitioner settings. This creates gaping holes in our understanding of 'what works for whom'. There is far more in the quantitative research literature on CBT than on humanistic therapies and couple therapies; there is more on depression than on obsessional thinking or pathological jealousy; there is more on majority than minority ethnic groups; and there is little on the elderly or people with learning disability. To add to this challenge, there is a vicious cycle in which therapies seen as having some evidence base – the ones on the NICE and EST lists – get most research funding, thus perpetuating the differentials.

ROM is a key corrective because it provides a way to ensure that therapies continue to evolve in an 'evidence-based' way and it also allows for data to accumulate on therapies that are not currently subject to large-scale outcome trials.

Myth 2: 'only randomised controlled trial evidence ascribes causality: that is what we need and all we need'

Talking of NICE and EST lists brings us to the second prevalent myth: the 'hierarchy of evidence', in which evidence from randomised controlled trials (RCTs) is seen to be of special and unique value. Different forms of evidence have different persuasive power and some are clearly more compelling and useful than others. However, in most fields of knowledge, different forms of evidence have complementary utility and cannot be organised into any one hierarchy. In geology, an extraordinary diversity of evidence is used to construct our understanding of how the planet has been shaped: simple visual mapping of rock types, identification of fossils, radiocarbon dating. Linguistics embraces laboratory experiments alongside historical attempts to construct the evolution of languages. Webs, not hierarchies, of evidence are the norm. We believe this model of what we term a 'web of evidence' better fits psychological therapies but is displaced by the myth of a single hierarchy of evidence. This mythical hierarchy is linked with a lack of discussion and understanding about the distinctions between research and routine OM, and between efficacy and effectiveness. If we are to have constructive critique of OM data, we have to unpack this.

Myth 2(a): randomisation gives causal attribution

Randomised controlled trials, in which different interventions are randomly delivered, are excellent for the evaluation of fertilisers and pest control treatments in agriculture, and much of the development of statistical methods to analyse RCT data came from that area. RCTs are also generally excellent in pharmacology, and it is unfortunate that therapies have been treated as if they were medication. What makes these application areas good for randomised trials is that fertilisers and plants cannot form ideas about whether they are getting the new or the old fertiliser, and in pharmacological RCTs great stress is placed on 'blinding' to ensure that patients cannot know what medication they are getting: they are 'blinded'. This is not always possible, but for most drug trials preparations can be created that are different but indistinguishable so the trial participants can be kept blind as to which group they are in.

Where people cannot be kept blind to what they receive, the 'placebo effect' kicks in. Placebo (Latin for 'I will please') refers to the psychological expectation that something will help. These are called 'expectancy effects' and are so powerful that they can impact on results, even on mortality, even when the 'something' is inert: a group who believe they are getting a new compound that helps them will have a better survival than those who think they are only getting something inert. The opposite of the placebo effects is the *nocebo* effect, which is the expectancy that something will be damaging. For example, people who are told that a treatment being offered in a trial may have negative side effects exhibit those side effects even if they are taking a sugar pill. This tells us something about how complex and sophisticated humans are: we are profoundly influenced by our expectations.

We are also social beings, and we communicate expectations to each other in subtle but powerful ways. The result of this is that there is overwhelming evidence that even when only the person delivering the preparation knows what it is, and does not tell the actual recipient, nevertheless the deliverer's knowledge still creates strong and statistically identifiable effects in the recipient.

To remove these effects in pharmacological RCTs, both the participants receiving the new or the old medication *and* the researchers delivering the preparations are kept in ignorance of which preparation is which. This is 'double-blinding' and only double-blind randomised controlled trials (DBRCTs) are accepted in the regulation of medicines (it is slightly more complex than this as not all drugs can be delivered blind, but this book is not about pharmacotherapies). In double-blind trials all expectancy effects are assumed to have been removed and any systematic difference between the drugs that is revealed when the outcome data are analysed is deemed to be due to the drug and not to expectancy effect.

This is all very sound, but no psychotherapy can be delivered single- or double-blind so we can never tease apart expectancies from 'real' effects in therapy RCTs. In fact, we must acknowledge that client and therapist expectancies are actually part of the power of therapies. Teasing out effects above and beyond those expectancies is logically impossible in our RCTs.

Let us be quite clear: we are staunch supporters of RCTs where this 'double-blinding' can be achieved. Then RCTs really do give causal attribution and are vital in assessing the relative effectiveness of drugs. They are rightfully a gold standard there. Let us also be clear: routine OM is just as contaminated with expectancy effects as are non-double-blind RCTs. The point we are making is that it is a myth to think that RCTs of therapies, which cannot even be single-blind, have some magic route to causal attribution; they simply do not.

Let us also be clear that the DBRCT, although a brilliant and apt tool in certain circumstances, such as pharmacology, is not unequivocally at the top of a general hierarchy of evidence even there. It is a valuable tool in order to be able to get new medication into use, although post-marketing surveillance is vital there too. The Thalidomide story reminds us why: a drug can pass the DBRCT hurdle and go into general use only to have to be withdrawn if evidence of unwanted effects accumulates from routine monitoring. This illustrates that pharmacological research does not have a single hierarchy of evidence; it draws on both RCTs and routine unwanted effect monitoring. This routine monitoring is designed to detect statistically significant associations, and these might only be present in a minority of patients or certain circumstances. In the case of Thalidomide, these were the birth defects in children that arose when the drug was taken during a particular phase of pregnancy.

It is unfortunate that this pharmacological twin approach has an asymmetry of 'good and bad' effects: DBRCTs look for evidence of positive effects to justify the drug being used, and routine 'post-market surveillance' looks for negative effects that may mean the drug must be withdrawn. In fact, were pharmacological post-market surveillance also designed to measure positive effects, we would have more detailed information about what is going on when some drugs work for some people and not for others, as appears to be the case for many drugs, specifically anti-depressants. That might help us to recognise that the two evidence sources form a complementary web, not a hierarchy. So strongly is therapy evaluation currently modelled on drug evaluation that if pharmacological post-marketing surveillance addressed positive outcomes, not just negative ones, ROM data might be seen in a much stronger light.

Myth 2(b): efficacy findings generalise to routine practice

Efficacy describes interventions carried out under ideal conditions with few interfering variables. Therapy efficacy studies are typically RCTs in which participants are selected who have one presenting problem and co-morbidity is avoided if at all possible. In efficacy studies, variables are rigidly defined and the context is tightly controlled. This is not the world of routine therapies. In routine work, many people come with 'co-morbidities', that is, they are struggling with more than one problem: an eating disorder *and* relationship problems; personality issues *and* a bereavement. We have already noted that systems for commissioning healthcare based essentially on RCT evidence make a logical error about causal attribution, given the issues about non-blindness in those RCTs. However, they make an equally important second logical mistake about generalisability.

To give a specific example from pharmacology, aspirin is a useful pain reliever that could, from large-scale trial data, be recommended for general use for headaches. However, such a generalisation ignores the fact that aspirin is contra-indicated for people with bleeding disorders. Fortunately, side effect monitoring shows this for aspirin, and additionally, some of the mechanisms that show aspirin works as a pain killer, as well as how it causes gastric bleeding, can be explored in laboratory experiments. By contrast, as we have very little real understanding of how therapies help, and even less about how they can sometimes harm, so we must explore the complexities and generalisability of therapy effects with process research and ROM data.

The generalisability of findings from efficacy studies to routine practice is an empirical question in itself and is not something that can be logically asserted without further evidence. We could argue that this puts ROM data above RCT evidence: only ROM data tell you about generalisability and its limitations. We strongly recommend the model of 'web of evidence' in which ROM data can replace over-valued assertions about RCT generalisability with empirical data. With time, we hope this recognition will lead to significant rethinking of research funding.

We have drawn heavily on medical and pharmacological examples here as these are the areas that have dominated empirical change measurement and therapy evaluation for the last half-century. However, we started with geology and linguistics, and our argument is that there are many areas of fertile study with no single hierarchy of evidence and in which no one has ever conducted an RCT: areas that recognise the importance of developing an interconnected "web of evidence".

Myth 3: 'there are lies, damned lies and statistics' and 'I can prove anything by statistics except the truth'

The first of the quotes is attributed to Mark Twain. While we disagree in part, we do acknowledge that the presentation of data in some of the psychotherapy change/outcomes literature is undoubtedly misleading, which brings us to the second quote, attributed to George Canning, with which we also disagree.

Now for the one new equation in this book (!):

statistics ≠ lies

For many practitioners, equations are as challenging or worse than tables of numbers or graphs. Perhaps that 'not equals' sign in our 'statistics ≠ lies' equation stirred some anxiety? For many practitioners who do not have a background in numbers or science, it can feel quite challenging to interpret change data, especially when it is reported statistically, and tempting to simply reject it altogether. Of course, as with any other tool, if inappropriate statistical procedures or measures are used, the results will be irrelevant, limited, misleading or frankly wrong: Quality in = Quality out, or more frankly, GIGO (Garbage in = Garbage out).

In Chapter 5, we introduced you to some common statistical procedures (*p* values, confidence intervals, reliable and significant change) so that you can digest the literature you read in a more informed way. However, we have not tried to teach statistics here – there are books that specifically do that and resources on the internet. What we want with this book is to encourage you to develop the confidence to have conversations about statistical issues with other practitioners, to ask questions and to generally feel more confident to detect common problems in arguments.

OK, after some myth-busting, we can move on in a less combative mode.

Section 2: There are no perfect models and no perfect OM data: creating constructive discussion

Moving on from the myths in section 1, we want to rehearse two common and problematic scenarios which you may recognise. We hope to give you some ideas about how to handle them:

1. You have some outcome data but someone is saying the data are worthless.
2. You are in a meeting in which someone is telling you that some data are definitively right and shows that what you are doing, clinically and/or in terms of your own data collection, is hopelessly wrong.

Stepping back from OMs for a minute, we believe that there is no particular approach or 'tool' for giving a complete understanding of what goes on in counselling or psychotherapy. This is no more or less true for OM data from therapies than it is for theoretical or clinical narratives. Each individual client's therapy is a unique, complex and personal journey. Not even the most enormous narrative case report can give a complete story of a single therapy, or even describe completely a single session.

Constructive critique starts with the recognition that any depiction of the 'outcome' of a therapy or change that has happened *must* be a very partial picture. We believe there are six useful principles and questions that can help you when negotiating the scenarios set out above.

Our six principles start with identifying and acknowledging two limitations that will be present in *any* evidence about change:

1. The partial picture means that there are some things that will not have been described or examined. That is just the nature of our field: it does not mean what *has* been described is worthless.
2. What has been described will never be described 'perfectly'. It may be but a pale and thin descriptor: a single number representing the entirety of someone's feeling of being down, or their 'quality of life'. It is thin, but again that does not mean it is worthless.

We go into more detail on those issues below. Our next two points look at what is useful in your evidence or data. We believe this always involves two assessments:

3. To what extent have the data presented addressed what the authors (people who collected the data) said they wanted to address?
4. To what extent do you think what is argued may be influenced by other things not measured or described (see #1 above)?

Finally, we recommend the 'surprise tests':

5. Did the data/evidence presented appear to have surprised those who are presenting it in some way?
6. Does something in the data surprise and interest you?

Those last two may be the same but they need not be: always try to check both. They may sound a bit subjective but remember, this how Penicillin was discovered. In the last section of this chapter, we unpack these six ideas more.

Section 3: constructing wise discussions of OM data

Accepting incompleteness

No one can collect all the evidence they would like to about their clinical work or expect someone else to do so on their behalf. Neither OM data, narrative transcriptions nor any other data collection can pretend to recreate the therapy. However, the fact of incompleteness can lead to people either not collecting any data at all, or else trying to collect too much in the mistaken belief this will better represent the therapy. Too much data can leave people overwhelmed such that the information never gets analysed or the key points get lost.

It may be useful to compare collection of data with photographs taken on a holiday. All such pictures, like all descriptions of change in therapy: (1) **are taken from one viewpoint**, (2) **omit much** and (3) **have imperfect descriptive quality**. But they do tell you something. Constructive critique recognises this and we recommend considering the points under the following headings.

1. Viewpoints: perspective and position

Just as a photograph is taken from a single point, all descriptions of change in therapy are selective. After a short time working with a client, we have learned enough about them to appreciate their uniqueness. This uniqueness is a combination of nomothetic and idiographic information about them. As we noted in Chapter 2, nomothetic descriptors are applicable to everyone: how tall, how anxious, how bitter, how articulate. Enough nomothetic information does start to map to just one person, but uniqueness is usually clinched by idiographic information, descriptors not shared with anyone else: the scar on the face that really is as unique as a fingerprint. In our field, more often, it is a psychological scar in the story of a relationship the client has now or has had in the past. We all process enormous volumes of information about everyone we meet.

In therapies, our theories help us to cope with the sheer volume of information we acquire about clients: theories help us to filter, summarise, prioritise, order and map the data. This simplifies things and our information is stored against templates: developmental or aetiological ideas, models that categorise ways in which we can help the client to change. This develops a picture from a particular viewpoint.

Every therapist stores and processes therapy information differently and what is available for recall is always simplified: even if sessions are video-recorded, replaying it misses the smell of the client, and it cannot record the associations and feelings that flashed through our minds in the session.

If someone is suggesting that you took your pictures from the wrong place, of the wrong things, at the wrong times, then the two of you almost certainly have different aims and aspirations. Step back from that and see if you can align more. All data reflect choices about perspective and position. Can you find *shared* interests? If someone is telling you their data are the only sort worth having, think about the reasons we select viewpoints. What might they acknowledge is missing from their data? Asking questions about what may be missing, offering ideas about what might complement, add to or improve their data, may help to find areas of common interests and allow you to move on, perhaps with an improved understanding.

2. Omissions and incomplete data

Choosing to use self-report change questionnaires means choosing which ones to use and deciding how often to use them (Chapters 2 to 5) and varies with how you work (Chapters 7 to 9). These choices define the deliberate omissions by the person collecting the data or by whoever commissioned the data. In our photograph metaphor, this is not only about what is outside the frame of the image, but also that different things will be included if you use a wide-angled lens or if you zoom into specific detail.

Clients also shape things and cause 'omissions'. They may choose not to fill in all, or even any, of the boxes in our questionnaires. If the client does not attend there will be no data from that day beyond the record of their non-attendance. All good and constructive critique recognises that there can be no complete set of data and that holes in the data will include both designed and uncontrollable, emergent losses. Good critique involves thinking about the impacts that omissions have on the picture but does not assume that such omissions are fatal. In fact, as with that non-attendance, omissions are data, albeit not what we wanted. Non-attendance is not a neutral process: it might be that the client really wanted the session but could not attend due to circumstances out of their control; or it could indicate non-engagement; or anger. Omissions in questionnaires should be thought about: they could suggest design issues with the questionnaire or the study; perhaps a questionnaire item about feeling life is not worth living is too exposing and it feels safer to miss it out.

So, as we keep emphasising, no dataset in our field can ever be so complete as to answer all important questions about therapy change and outcome. However, discussing what is missing can help to mitigate overly definite claims. Reporting omissions helps other researchers to know how generalisable the results might be. One important omission that is very common in our field is that of short follow-up periods. If your last data collection point is at the final session of a therapy, then clearly this omits the rest of the client's life. This is a very early 'outcome'.

Equally importantly, scores on this occasion may be impacted by all sorts of feelings the client had about ending the treatment. Having a data collection point a few weeks later can minimise those immediacy effects. Having a data collection point some substantial time later - six months, a year, even two years on - will tell you something very important about whether any change was sustained. Of course, for any client there are all sorts of things that can happen in such a follow-up time and so we cannot say that the change was necessarily down to the therapy. But if we can find ways to collect follow-up data, we will learn about outcomes. Follow-up is not traditional in our field and is subject to many challenges. One sad but real challenge is that the proportion of clients who will complete measures tends to fall off markedly with time from the end of therapy, so, at least with our current approaches, the omission of longer follow-up will be a mix of us not even seeking it, and proportions of clients opting out of it when we do. However, this is one of the omissions in our field we can try to address.

If your own data are being criticised as incomplete, it may be helpful to separate whether that criticism is being used in an attempt to completely reject the data or can help us to learn from the critique. We find it useful to consider:

- Do we and the critic have different aims and interests? For example, were we mainly interested in overall outcomes and the critic keen to learn about individual change trajectories to inform embedded change management? Were we mainly interested in demographic factors that might affect change and the critic mainly interested in the number of sessions attended?
- Were our omissions avoidable? Could this usefully be revised in future data collection?
- Do our omissions genuinely invalidate claims being made about the data or is it more that they simply give rise to questions?

Being open and transparent about omissions in reporting allows for this kind of constructive dialogue.

3. Descriptive quality

No picture has perfect quality. Low resolution, distorted colour reproduction or limited contrast range can all reduce the ability of a photograph to convey the image sought. However, sometimes reduced quality can convey a clearer picture or reveal something unexpected: a black and white photograph may convey more clearly the beauty of a scene than a colour photograph. Similarly, descriptions of change using OMs will vary in quality. A short questionnaire will probably cover fewer areas of possible change than a longer one and will also offer a reduced range of possible scores. However, it may be more likely that clients will complete it regularly and often (and it can be supplemented by a longer one, less frequently). This may be like moving from rich but unaffordable colour to multiple lower resolution but more digestible black and white images.

The statistical summaries we discussed in Chapter 5 - means, SDs and estimates of effects - are also choices about quality. They are useful summaries, but not magical ends in themselves. As always, the value of any data is dependent on the quality of discourse surrounding it, including discussion of the appropriateness of the measures or methods of analysis chosen. The value always comes from evaluating the techniques you used and comparing them with alternatives that were not chosen.

One aspect of this 'descriptive quality' is the difference between idiographic and nomothetic change/outcome measures. An idiographic client-generated measure such as PSYCHLOPS (Chapter 4) will almost certainly provide a better focus on what the client considers are their problems than a nomothetic measure will. However, it must lose comparability with scores from other clients. The photo metaphor is stretched here, but it is like the client taking idiosyncratic selfies - the picture from their chair will be different from any other client's selfie.

How do we assess the 'quality' of a descriptor? This takes us back to the 'psychometric parameters', the different measures of reliability and forms of and measures of validity that we introduced in Chapter 3. These can be excellent indicators of the quality of change data but they are often misused and given 'gold standard' status that may not be correct for their purpose as OMs.

Reliability and validity

Reliability

As noted in Chapter 3, internal reliability and test-retest reliability, if used sensibly, can be very useful guides when evaluating OMs, and inter-rater reliability is important when choosing OMs based on observer ratings. However, unlike the reliability of a weighing scales or a thermometer, reliability of therapy OMs won't necessarily generalise from one sample to another and it should not be over-valued. A short questionnaire with internal reliability of .7 may be better than a long measure with reliability of .98 if the long measure is so long that clients will baulk at repeating it: be wary of condemnation of a measure for having only middling reliability. Similarly, when a study reports the reliability for a measure, you should question where that reliability was established and its generalisability. For example, reliability established with a group of university students may well not generalise to an older adult population or to a group of asylum seekers. All OM measurement should report internal reliability computed from the actual data when multi-item measures are used. That way, no generalisation from reliability observed in another sample is involved at all.

Validity

As with reliability, we would like indicators of validity for the OMs we use and those used in any report that interests us. However, as we noted in Chapter 3, validity has various aspects, including construct, convergent, divergent and predictive validities. This means that an OM may have different validity depending on the criterion: a questionnaire measure may have high convergent validity with another questionnaire measure of the same focus but markedly lower convergent validity against an observer rating of the same issue. Statistics for validity are not absolute tests – the psychological issues we are measuring are too complex for that. This also means that we only have quite limited explorations of validity for most therapy OMs. This makes the validity descriptors we do have valuable but rarely sufficient to say that one measure is unequivocally better than another. Much will depend on the particular client group and use of the data.

Because of these complexities, we recommend just two rules for psychometric critique:

1. Be wary when limited validity exploration is used to judge an OM. The blanket assertions either that an OM 'is a validated measure' or the attack that one is 'not validated' are naïve.
2. Be wary of assertions equating validity with a clean factor structure or attacking short general measures that lack such a factor structure as invalid. This is a misunderstanding of the method (see Chapter 3).

Avoiding the war of words and honing abstruse words into sharp swords

All professions and specialisms adopt their own language that includes specialist words and terminologies. These words are often necessary to simplify communication and can reduce ambiguities. However, terminology can be used to alienate people and establish 'in-groups'. All therapy modalities have their own specialist words, some perhaps more so than others. Similarly, quantitative data analysts have their own words, and although generally we feel they were created and shaped by genuine necessity, they can still be used to scare people off. In Chapters 3 and 5, we have tried to use the words and concepts we think are useful or essential, and to give an explanation of them in as plain language as we can. As with therapeutic language, sometimes ordinary words are taken hostage ('self', 'identity', 'projection', 'reliability', 'validity', 'average') and some are just exotic ('humanism', 'transpersonal', 'transference', 'interquartile range', 'null hypothesis'). Some do both. They take the ordinary and overload it in a very particular way to flaunt the exotic nature of the knowledge: 'regression' is a word hijacked both by some therapists and by statisticians.

There are no quick or easy answers to prevent words being used as swords or magical shields, but we hope that having read this book you will feel more confidence to question alienating language: technical language can become a misuse of power and be intimidatory. When you have time, referring to our online glossary (ombook.psyctc.org/glossary/) and back to particular chapters should help, but in face-to-face encounters we hope you will feel confident enough to ask the other person to try to explain what they meant if a word is alien or feels more like a weapon than a tool. It is reasonable to expect experts to try to explain things in a way that a genuinely interested person from another speciality can understand. Asking for this politely can disarm the weaponised language which is common around therapy OMs.

Using the (metaphorical) internet to put the photo in context

If we are trying to avoid the 'you're wrong, I'm right' discourses around OM data, what should we seek to have in its place? One of the remarkable changes of the last 20–30 years has been the radical growth in information available on the internet. Let us go back to our photo metaphor: given some geographical location, it is now possible, when looking at a photograph from somewhere you have never visited, to find other images of it, maps or even an aerial view of it. Different maps may be available that highlight different aspects of the place. In addition, we can often find narratives and numeric information about a place that put the photo in context. Exploring these different perspectives helps us to think more flexibly and to notice what may be missing in the photo.

There is a similar process to finding out more about any report of therapy change/outcome, often, again, using the internet. We can usually find out about the authors and their affiliations, their areas of expertise and preferences. We can check words and concepts that we are not sure we understood. There are some excellent online videos and talks that explain statistics in simple terms. We can usually find out about OMs if we do not know them.

However, even more important than literal use of the internet, we believe it is part of the discourse about OM data to ask questions that seek to put any report in context. Such exploration should not seek to accept the report without question, nor should it be an attempt to destroy any value in it. Rather, using collateral information should help us to a better understanding of the inevitable effects we have summarised as arising from (1) viewpoint, (2) omissions and (3) distortions.

Where does the truth lie? Veracity/integrity

We think it is useful, if a bit dangerously binary, to ask to what extent any description of therapy is 'truthfully reported'. This can be like a court process of deciding if someone is a credible and unbiased witness. One important consideration in reading any narrative case report of therapy is not just about the quality of the methodology, but is also a more human, motivational, judgement: Does the narrative ring true to you? How did the obligation to ensure anonymity restrict things? How might conscious or unconscious factors have caused the authors to have distorted things? Was there a desire of the authors to prove their own perspective that impacted on the methodology? Perhaps those questions should always be 'how much has...?' and not just 'has...?'. Starting there, we can then ask if anything has fundamentally compromised the veracity and integrity of the report. Sometimes reports leak clues about the selection and distortion of information, although this may be simply impossible to assess without further material.

Similar issues apply as much to reports of quantitative data as to qualitative ones and, sadly, there have been cases where data have been fabricated by researchers. More often, data are omitted without transparent declaration of why this was done; or results may be analysed in very particular ways that replace the original designed analysis; or data may be 'dredged' or 'mined' for any finding that is 'significant', even in the absence of any original idea or hypothesis as to why this might be expected to be the case. Where this happens, the generalisability - replicability - of the finding is likely to be low or zero and the practice is frankly dishonest. It seems highly probable that the increasing pressures on those seeking academic or research careers to publish a lot of work, to get cited a lot, and to bring in big research grants, often drive people to these unethical practices. There is no entirely reliable or valid way to detect research fraud. To a limited extent, good peer reviewing of publications in journals helps. Methodological guidelines help reviewers, editors and readers to be sure things have not been omitted or to show where the omissions were. The CONSORT rules for trials have been influential and have improved trial methods, and now the expectation that any trial should be declared in a public trial registry is slowly improving trial transparency. The most recent development that should improve honesty is 'open data', where researchers place their data in publicly accessible repositories so that analyses can be checked. Clearly, with OM data great care must be taken that open data cannot leak identities of participants. The online companion to this chapter has more information about CONSORT, registries and data repositories. Currently, there are no such guidelines or registers for ROM, and as ROM can be far more diverse than trial design, such frameworks will take time to evolve. However, a little critical wariness will remain an essential tool for critical appreciation of accounts of change in therapy.

Equipoise in clinical and research setting

One crucial idea in research, and certainly in the 'analytic attitude' or 'therapeutic stance' in the clinical setting, is of holding equipoise: that is, trying to hold an evenly balanced view or neutrality in appraising information. Sometimes we wonder if a definition of 'neutrality' from systemic theory might help. That definition is that neutrality was achieved if the family could not agree at the end of the session whose side you were on. Whenever you are reading a report or paper it is helpful to wonder about what the vested interests of the writers might be. Is it likely that all readers agree 'which side the authors were on'? If so, perhaps we should be very cautious about the reporting.

Equally, we should be striving to achieve some sort of equipoise and to avoid being driven by our own vested interests or long-held beliefs as we digest and critique such work. Complete neutrality is not possible for the reasons we have described throughout this chapter and because this work is a human endeavour. Being open to exploring our and others' biases means we can work with them rather than ignore them.

Summary and final conclusion

In this chapter we have tried to draw together themes that have been present throughout the book to encourage a reflective, enquiring but also critical view of your own plans to carry out ROM, but also to help you to understand, digest and challenge constructively others' work. A constructively critical approach to OM data is essential if we are to create bodies of evidence that are fit for purpose and help to improve both our methods and our understanding of what matters to our clients. It is only by working in this way that we can build creative conversations between therapists, clients commissioners, researchers and statisticians. In the famous words of E. M. Forster, 'Only Connect!'

References

American Psychological Association (2021) *Empirially Supported Treatments*. [online] Available at: https://div12.org/psychological-treatments/ [Accessed 19 May 2021].

Beck, A. T., Steer, R. A., & Garbin, M. G. (1988) Psychometric properties of the Beck Depression Inventory: Twenty-five years of evaluation. *Clinical Psychology Review, 8*(1), 77–100.

Beck, A. T., Ward, C. H., Mendelson, M., Mock, J., & Erbaugh, J. (1961) An inventory for measuring depression. *Archives of General Psychiatry, 4*, 561–571.

Bohr, N. (1963) *Essays 1958-1962 on Atomic Physics and Human Knowledge*. Interscience Publishers: New York.

Chapman, R. (2021) *LightBulb Cartoon – Home*. [online] Lightbulbcartoon.com. Available at: http://lightbulbcartoon.com/ [Accessed 5 February 2021].

Child Outcomes Research Consortium (CORC) (2021) *Outcome & Experience Measures*. [online] Available at: www.corc.uk.net/outcome-experience-measures/ [Accessed 4 February 2021].

CORE and CORE System Trust (CST) (2021) *Information about the CORE-OM – CORE and CORE System Trust (CST)*. [online] Available at: www.coresystemtrust.org.uk/instruments/core-om-information/ [Accessed 4 February 2021].

Hamilton, M. (1960) A rating scale for depression. *Journal of Neurology, Neurosurgery & Psychiatry, 23*, 56–62. Available at: https://dcf.psychiatry.ufl.edu/files/2011/05/HAMILTON-DEPRESSION.pdf/ [Accessed 4 February 2021].

Keats, J. (1819) 'Ode on a Grecian Urn' by John Keats. [online] Poetry Foundation. Available at: www.poetryfoundation.org/poems/44477/ode-on-a-grecian-urn [Accessed 4 February 2021].

National Institute for Mental Health in England (2008) *Outcomes Compendium: Helping you select the right tools for best mental health care practice in your field*. Department of Health. Available at: http://webarchive.nationalarchives.gov.uk/20130107105354/http://www.dh.gov.uk/prod_consum_dh/groups/dh_digitalassets/documents/digitalasset/dh_093677.pdf [Accessed 19 May 2021].

NHS Digital (2021) *National Clinical Content Repository (Copyright Licensing Service) – NHS Digital*. [online] Available at: https://digital.nhs.uk/services/national-clinical-content-repository-copyright-licensing-service [Accessed 4 February 2021].

NICE (2021) *NICE Guidance*. [online] Available at: https://www.nice.org.uk/guidance [Accessed 19 May 2021].

OQ Measures (2021) *OQ®-45.2 – OQ Measures*. [online] Available at: www.oqmeasures.com/oq-45-2/ [Accessed 4 February 2021].

Patient Health Questionnaire (PHQ) (n.d.) *Screeners*. [online] Available at: www.phqscreeners.com/ [Accessed 4 February 2021].

Psychological Outcome Profiles (n.d.) *Psychological Outcome Profiles – PSYCHLOPS*. [online] Available at: http://psychlops.org.uk/ [Accessed 4 February 2021].

PSYCTC.org (2021) *Body Shape Questionnaire (BSQ)*. [online] Available at: www.psyctc.org/psyctc/psyctc-org-home/instruments/body-shape-questionnaire-bsq/ [Accessed 4 February 2021].

Stern, A. (2014) The Hospital Anxiety and Depression Scale. *Occupational Medicine*, *64*(5), 393–394. Available at: https://academic.oup.com/occmed/article/64/5/393/1436876 [Accessed 4 February 2021].

xkcd - Appliances. [online] Available at: https://xkcd.com/ [Accessed 5 February 2021].

Index

Kolibri 360 GmbH
Ferdinand-Jühlke-Straße 7
99095 Erfurt, Deutschland
produktsicherheit@kolibri360.de